Megalithic Builders of South India

Archaeo-Anthropological Investigations on Human Skeletal Remains from Kodumanal

Megalithic Builders of South India

Archaeo-Anthropological Investigations on Human Skeletal Remains from Kodumanal

Veena Mushrif-Tripathy • K. Rajan • S.R. Walimbe

Indira Gandhi Rashtriya Manav Sangrahalaya
Bhopal

Centre for Ancient Human Skeletal Studies
Pune

Aryan Books International
New Delhi

Megalithic Builders of South India:
Archaeo-Anthropological Investigations on
Human Skeletal Remains from Kodumanal

ISBN: 978-81-7305-410-5

Published in **2011** by

INDIRA GANDHI RASHTRIYA MANAV SANGRAHALAYA
Shamla Hills, Bhopal - 462 013 (M.P.)

and

CENTRE FOR ANCIENT HUMAN SKELETAL STUDIES
28, Ideal Colony, Matoshri Sulabha Society, Paud Road,
Kothrud, Pune - 411 029 (India)

and

ARYAN BOOKS INTERNATIONAL
Pooja Apartments, 4B, Ansari Road, New Delhi - 110 002 (India)
Tel.: 23287589, 23255799; Fax: 91-11-23270385
E-mail: aryanbooks@vsnl.com, aryanbooks@gmail.com
www.aryanbooks.co.in

Computer Typeset and Printed in India at
ABI Prints & Publishing Co., New Delhi

Foreword

In common parlance, heritage is construed as human-made and cultural, although human biological heritage is as important as the cultural heritage. Archaeologists and palaeo-anthropologists sometimes find ancient bones from their excavations, which constitute the precious human biological heritage. This is because of the fact that these skeletal remains precisely indicate age, sex, general physical characteristics, genetic traits and pathology of the ancient populations. It is also possible to carry out increasingly sophisticated scientific tests on skeletal remains, such as dietary analysis, DNA sequencing, age estimation, dating, etc. to acquire further knowledge on the ancient populations. The present volume on human skeletal remains from Kodumanal in Tamil Nadu is another addition to the existing scant resources on the subject. The authors claim that in this study they had deviated from the conventional research strategy of ending up with "racial" classification of the ancient population by adopting a more promising "bio-cultural perspective" to trace the progress of human evolution and adaptation. Moreover, the site selected for this study is one of the best excavated, best attended and best reported Megalithic-Early Historic sites, where the skeletal remains are in a fairly good state of preservation.

This book is the outcome of a landmark study in more than one respect. It has attempted to open a new window to know more about the Megalithic and Early Historic populations of the peninsular region of India. It contributes immensely to the debate on phenotypic homogeneity versus variations of the Indian Megalithic and Iron Age populations by reaffirming the hypothesis that variability is more pronounced in these populations than homogeneity. It also concludes that there is no biological proof to support the invasion of foreign people into the southern Deccan with the introduction of iron technology. This study sheds light on palaeo-pathological scrutiny of skeletal and dental remains. It conclusively establishes high rate of infant mortality, optimum life expectancy around 30-35 years, lack of major infectious pathology, etc. among the early populations around Kodumanal. Another significant finding of the study is the lack of major traumatic lesion in the skulls excavated from Kodumanal, whereas such cases are rampant in other sites of the region. From whatever little evidence that is available from Kodumanal, the authors have suggested that since the victims survived for a few days after the skull injury, possibly the Iron Age population of the region had the knowledge and skill to treat such serious injuries. The study also indicates occupation-related problems, such as air pollution in the kitchen or near the furnace that might have led to lesion of maxillary sinusitis. These and other similar findings make the book more interesting and worthy of a serious perusal.

My sincere thanks are due to the authors for their extremely painstaking study and valuable contribution to the area of ancient skeletal research. This publication was possible due to the efforts made by my colleagues at the Indira Gandhi Rashtriya Manav Sangrahalaya (IGRMS) and M/s Aryan Books International, for which I am grateful to all of them. I hope, this book would be of great help to the students and researchers in palaeo-anthropology in general and ancient skeletal study in particular.

Kamal K. Misra
Director, IGRMS

Preface

It is our great pleasure to bring out the report on the studies on human skeletal remains recovered from the site of Kodumanal.

Human skeletal remains offer a fruitful subject of inquiry in archaeology. Unless the bodily structures and health of the members of a community are studied no social reconstruction is complete. Skeletal remains afford valuable information on age at death, sex of the deceased, cause of mortality, bone injuries and certain diseases present in the population. This helps draw demographic structure of the population, i.e. age and sex proportions, mortality rates, morbidity pattern, life expectancy, etc. The effect of climate, ecology and inherited gene complex on human physiology can also be inferred. However, studies on human skeletons are largely neglected in Indian archaeology. As a result, the research potential of the excavated human skeletons remains grossly under-utilized.

Primary objective in forming the Centre for Ancient Human Skeletal Studies is to promote the subject in the region. Besides undertaking independent and collaborative research activities that concern bio-cultural understanding of protohistoric or contemporary human evolution-migration-variation, the Centre is proposing to bring out a series of publications in this line of research. This research marks the first publication of the Centre in this series, jointly undertaken with the Indira Gandhi Rashtriya Manav Sangrahalaya, Bhopal and Aryan Books International, New Delhi.

The report on the Kodumanal human skeletal series is important in many ways. The site of Kodumanal is one of the best excavated, best attended, and best reported Early Historic-Megalithic sites of the Indian peninsular region. The skeletal remains were in fairly good state of preservation, and more importantly made available for detailed anthropological study. The report deviates from the conventional anthropological design, but, follows the bio-cultural approach which provides information on many important facets of this bygone population. For the first time in Indian archaeology the human remains recovered from the excavation are not looked as isolated pieces of evidence for mere description of bodily features, but anthropologists and the excavator are joining hands while interpreting the biological features in terms of literary, epigraphical and archaeological data. We hope that this humble attempt will be well received in the discipline.

Archaeological excavations at the habitation-cum-burial site of Kodumanal were undertaken by the Department of Epigraphy and Archaeology, Tamil University, Thanjavur, under the leadership of Prof. Y. Subbarayalu. Collaborating agencies for the excavation were the Department of Ancient History and Archaeology, Madras University and the Tamil Nadu State Archaeology Department. The second author was closely associated with the excavation and the associated studies all the way through, and has mainly been concerned with research reporting on archaeological findings. Studies on the human skeletal series were undertaken by the first author during 2000-02 under the supervision of the third author.

This research would not have been possible without financial support and co-operation of many organizations. The authors sincerely thank the University Grants Commission and the Tamil University for the financial support. The laboratory studies were undertaken at the Anthropology Laboratory of the Deccan College Post-Graduate and Research Institute, Pune by the first and the third author during their association with this Institute. The authors express their sincere thanks to Deccan College and Tamil University authorities for allowing use of the infrastructural facilities while undertaking this study. They also express sincere gratitude to all scholars, students and staff members of these organizations for the co-operation and assistance offered by them during the course of this research.

Publication of this report is possible with the financial support of the Indira Gandhi Rashtriya Manav Sangrahalaya, Bhopal, and logistic support of Aryan Books International, New Delhi. We personally thank Prof. Kamal K. Misra, Director IGRMS and Shri Vikas Arya, M/s Aryan Books International for their interest in this research.

Veena Mushrif-Tripathy
K. Rajan
S.R. Walimbe

Contents

List of Illustrations

1

Kodumanal: Archaeological Settings

The site of Kodumanal is situated ($11^0 6'$ 42" N; $77^0 30'$ 51" E) in the semi-arid region, on the north bank of the river Noyyal, a tributary of Kaveri, in Perundurai Taluka of Erode district, Tamil Nadu (Fig. 1.1). It is ideally situated on the ancient trade route connecting Karur, the Chera capital of Sangam Age on the confluence of river Amaravathi with river Kaveri, with the Musiri port on west coast through the Palghat gap (Fig. 1.2). The Sangam literature, *Patirrupattu* referred to this site as *Kodumanam* (*Patirruppattu* poem 67 and 74) and also as bead making centre. The available archaeological sites within the vicinity of Kodumanal suggest its cultural importance (Fig. 1.3).

Archaeological excavations at the habitation-cum-burial site of Kodumanal were undertaken by Y. Subbarayalu and K. Rajan, the second author of the book, of the Department of Epigraphy and Archaeology, Tamil University, Thanjavur, during the years 1985, 1986, 1989 and 1990 (Figs. 1.4 and 1.5). Collaborating agencies for the excavation were the Department of Ancient History and Archaeology, Madras University and the Tamil Nadu State Archaeology Department. The Tamil Nadu State Archaeology Department re-excavated the site in the years 1998 and 1999 (Rajan 1999).

During the course of excavation, forty-eight trenches were laid in the habitation area and thirteen Early Historic megalithic burials were opened in the cemetery area (Fig. 1.6). The excavation showed that the cemetery belongs to the late phase of the Megalithic period, and was used by people living in nearby habitation. The inscribed Tamil-Brahmi potsherds were collected from the lowermost level habitation, which clearly indicates that

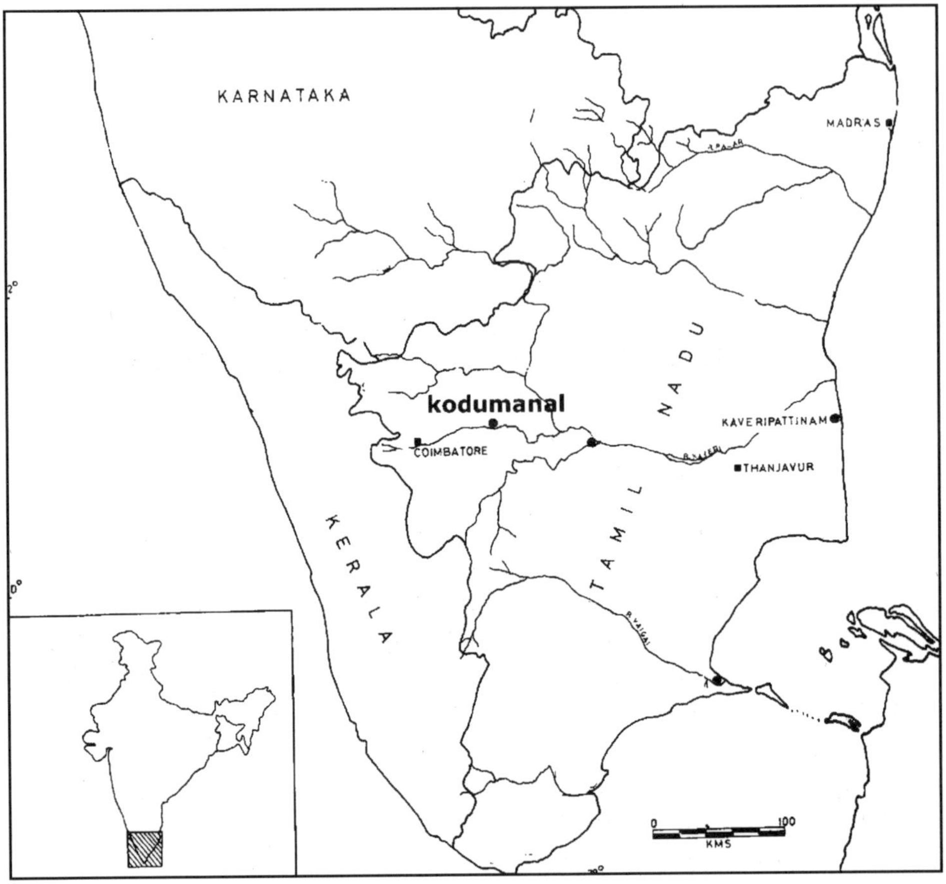

Fig. 1.1 Approximate location of the Kodumanal site.

it already entered into the Early Historic period. Quite interestingly, an inscribed potsherd reading *visaki* was collected from a transepted cist with passage on the east enclosed by cairn-circle with a menhir planted on the periphery. It clearly indicates that the Megalithic burials excavated at this site in fact entered into the Early Historic period very much. Otherwise, one may say that this site is an Early Historic site with a follower of the cist burial system. *However, the periodization that followed in the previous publications by the excavator Y. Subbarayalu is followed here to avoid confusion with the previous and present one.*[1]

It yielded extensive data on the nature of settlement, gemstone industry, method of iron and steel production, weaving and shell industry, type of burials and their architectural features, the types and placement of grave goods, the mode of burial, the usage of graffiti marks and Brahmi

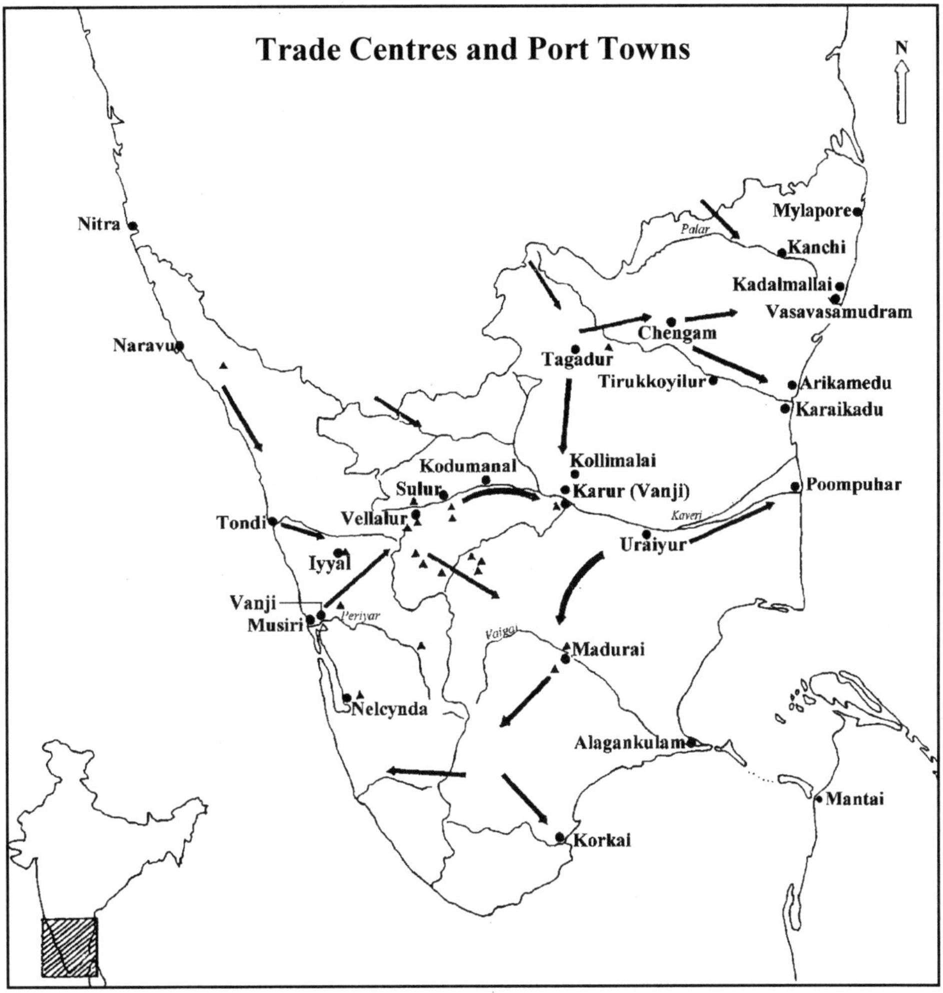

Fig. 1.2 Trade centres and routes in relation to Kodumanal.

characters, the stratigraphical position of the russet-coated painted ware (russet-coated ware) and punch-marked coins (PMC), the extent of internal and external trade and interrelated topics (for more details, see Rajan 1990, 1991, 1996, 1999).

STRATIGRAPHY

The oldest part of the habitation has a deposit of 2 m, whereas other parts have only 1 m deposit. On the basis of cultural material, ceramics and palaeography of the Brahmi letters, the deposit is divided into two cultural periods, namely, Megalithic period and Early Historical period datable

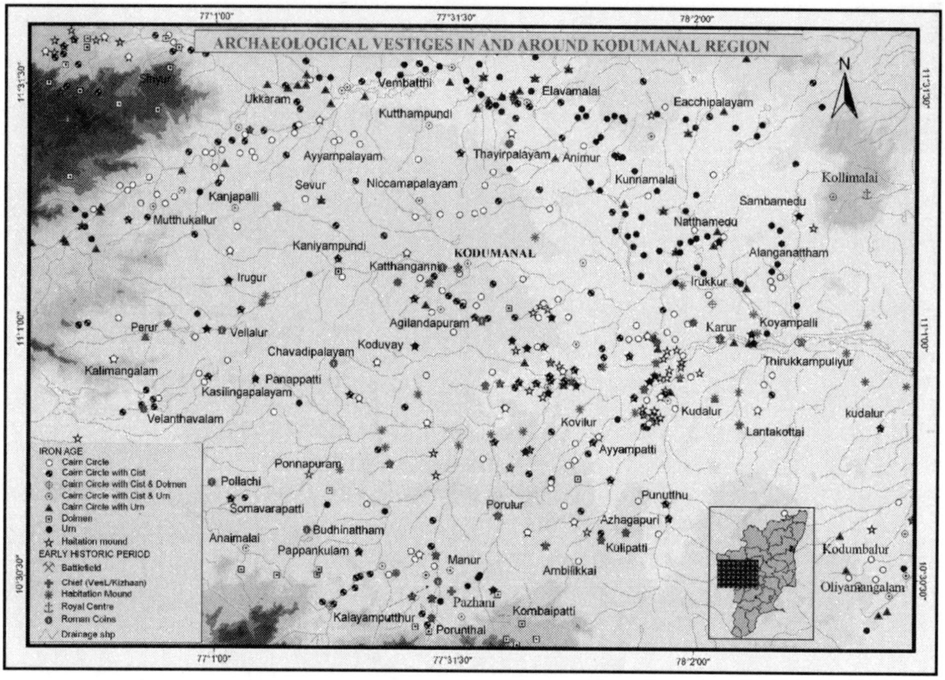

Fig. 1.3 Archaeological vestiges in and around Kodumanal.

respectively to 400 BC-AD 100 and AD 100-AD 300. Period I, the Megalithic period, is further divided into sub-period IA and IB. The people of the first period were mostly artisans working on semi-precious stones, particularly rock crystal and carnelian, and the people of the second period were generally cultivators. The statistical analysis of the pottery collected from the different strata of the nine groups of trenches yielded a very significant role of russet-coated painted white kaolin ware (russet-coated ware). It is found that in the lower levels, the russet-coated ware on the one hand and plain black and red ware on the other are to be found in almost equal proportions and all the pottery looks bright and polished. Dull or unslipped red ware occurs in equal proportion to red polished ware. In the middle levels, the painted ware decreases while plain ware increases. Moreover, also common are comparatively thicker storage vessels in black and red ware. The red ware shows an increase in number but black and red ware is still the dominant type. In the upper levels, i.e., from Layer 3 upwards, red ware predominates. Though black and red ware lingers, it appears dull and lacks its earlier luster.

Fig. 1.4 General view of habitation.

Fig. 1.5 General view of graveyard.

Fig. 1.6 General view of grave.

The time range when the black and red ware is dominant may be classified as a distinct period with two sub-periods IA and IB. Period IA is the one when russet-coated ware is predominantly used and IB is that when it becomes less prominent. Layers 7 and 8 from 140 cm-190 cm are thus assigned to subperiod IA, and layers 4 to 6 measuring from 60 cm to 140 cm are assigned to IB. The upper three layers, i.e., from the surface down to 60 cm belong to Period II.

This division of the deposit into two periods is also supported by other cultural material. In Period I, beads made of semi-precious stones and rock crystal, potsherds bearing graffiti marks and Brahmi letters, a crucible furnace, an iron smelting furnace and the russet-coated ware occur in greater numbers than in Period II where terracotta and glass objects, storage pits, red ware, etc. dominate the deposit. This may suggest that during the earlier period, the emphasis was more on exploiting natural resources such as semi-precious stones and iron ore deposits.

SETTLEMENT

The eight trenches opened in the mid part of the habitation mound yielded a maximum number of eight floors, of which the earlier five belong to the

Megalithic period. The square/rectangular gravel-paved floors plastered with lime were generally oriented north-south. The associate postholes dug into the periphery of the floors were found with sand. The absence of tiles and occurrence of a few brick-bats suggested the thatched roof. In a few trenches, in place of postholes the base of a wall made of gravel was found. Even today, the use of lime plaster on the floor and red gravel for the construction of walls continues locally.

The two floors of the bottom levels yielded round bins and might have served as raised platforms to support the grain storage vessels. The situation, however, was reversed in Period II, where a small circular pit dug into the soil neatly trimmed and lined with bricks was used to store grain. Similar elaborately built storage pits can be observed in this region.

The nature of floor level, availability of the antiquities, iron and crucible furnace, semi-precious stone chips, etc. clearly indicate that during the Megalithic period, the artisans mainly manufacturing steel and semi-precious stone beads were concentrated in the northern zone of the habitation whereas the agriculturist in the central zone and agriculturists as well as the people involved in the iron industry occupied the southern part of the habitation.

IRON AND STEEL INDUSTRY

An interesting and remarkable achievement of these people was in the production of iron and steel. The evidence for this industry was found in two groups of trenches 300 m apart from each other and situated respectively on the southern and northern part of the habitation mound. The Megalithic iron ores are extensively used at this site as iron smelting is found in and around Chennimalai hill, the offshoot of Salem range, which lies about 15 km east of Kodumanal.

The data collected from the resistivity survey made in the iron slag scattered area of about 100 sq.m on the southern edge of the habitation mound suggested the concentration of furnaces. One of the three trenches laid at this place yielded a circular base (115 cm dia.) of a furnace at a depth of 65 cm right on the natural soil (Fig. 1.7). This circular portion was distinguished by white colour, caused perhaps due to high temperature. Around this circular base, numerous iron slags, burnt clay embedded with slag, vitrified brick-bats, many tuyere pieces (terracotta pipes) with vitrified mouth and a granite slab were collected. Some of the iron slags stuck to the wall portion of the furnace had a smooth surface. The available tuyeres 15 cm in length, 6 cm in thickness and with a hole of

Fig. 1.7 Iron smelting furnace.

1.5 cm in diameter suggest that the bellows were used quite near to the furnace. The granite slabs found near the furnace seem to have been used for forging. Since the furnaces were dismantled to remove the bloom after smelting, it is hard to get the furnace intact. The absence of postholes, floor level, mere occurrence of potsherds and absence of any antiquities in this smelting area suggest that iron smelting was done on the periphery of the habitation.

CRUCIBLE FURNACE

Fifteen trenches laid 300 m north of the above-said iron smelting area yielded two crucible furnaces of which one is found in unused condition. A large, somewhat oval-shaped, main furnace surrounded by more than 12 small furnaces was exposed on the bottom most level at a depth of 125 cm (Fig. 1.8). The big furnace measured 112 cm north-south and 100 cm east-west with a depth of 40 cm. The burnt clay wall was 20 cm in thickness. Inside the furnace pit were collected burnt clay pieces with rectangular holes. The pieces were obviously part of the furnace wall. The holes allowed the air to pass through evenly into the furnace. The complete

Fig. 1.8 Steel-making crucible furnace.

absence of the tuyeres in the crucible furnace suggests that these holes were arranged for a natural draft of air into the furnace.

The small circular furnaces surrounding this big furnace, almost at regular intervals, had 30 cm diameter at the mouth with a small hole or depression in the centre. These might have been used to heat longer crucibles removed from bigger one. The important find here is a vitrified crucible, partially broken, found in the small furnace *in situ* position. This small bowl-shaped crucible had a diameter of 9 cm at the mouth with total thickness of 0.7 cm at the top and 0.9 cm at the base. Besides these, many fragmentary pieces of vitrified crucibles were also found. Another interesting find is an unused crucible furnace and a crucible made of well levigated clay.

GEMSTONE INDUSTRY

Besides the manufacture of iron and steel, another important economic mainstay of these people was the gemstone industry. The area is known for its semi-precious stones. The famous beryl-bearing site Padiyur and sapphire-bearing hillocks Sivanmalai and Perumalmalai lie about 15 km south and south-east respectively of Kodumanal. A quartz-bearing site Vengamedu (*venga* means quartz and *medu* means mound) and Arasampalayam lie 5 km north and south respectively of Kodumanal. Besides, another small quartz-bearing mound is also observed a kilometre north of the habitation mound. The usage of the huge quart blocks as part of the circle clearly suggests that it had been fully exploited during the days of the site itself. The absence of raw materials like carnelian and lapis-lazuli in this region suggests that these have been imported from Gujarat-Maharashtra and Afghanistan, respectively.

Beads of sapphire, beryl, agate, carnelian, amethyst, lapis-lazuli, jasper, garnet, soapstone and quartz were unearthed from the habitation whereas beads of carnelian, particularly the etched variety, and agate were restricted to burials. For instance, Meg.II yielded 80 carnelian beads, Meg.V about 2220 and Meg.X about 1000. The occurrence of 2220 carnelian beads in a single burial may be the first instance of its kind in India. The amount of beads collected from 13 burials out of 150 survived burials alone indicates the intensity of the trade activities that had taken place between the north and south.

The beads in different manufacturing stages, finished and semi-finished, drilled and undrilled, polished and unpolished, were unearthed along with the raw material. The discarded chips, grooved stone slab and an interesting stone slab with few grooved beads intact clearly demonstrate that these were manufactured locally at Kodumanal. The survival of this age-old tradition could be seen at Kangayam, the nearby town. The ethno-archaeological study carried out in Kangayam region by the second author clearly shows that the present day traditional bead-making artisans are still following the same old method that one observed in Kodumanal.

WEAVING INDUSTRY

The occurrence of quite a number of intact terracotta spindle whorls pierced at the centre by means of an iron rod is clearly suggestive of cotton processing. To strengthen this fact, a remarkably well-preserved piece of woven cotton was recovered from the site.

GRAFFITI

The habitation part of the site yielded a number of graffiti-bearing potsherds. Most of them were recovered from the earlier and middle levels. It is found that half of the graffiti that could be recognized consists of various signs and geometric pattern and the other half consists of clearly recognizable Brahmi letters.

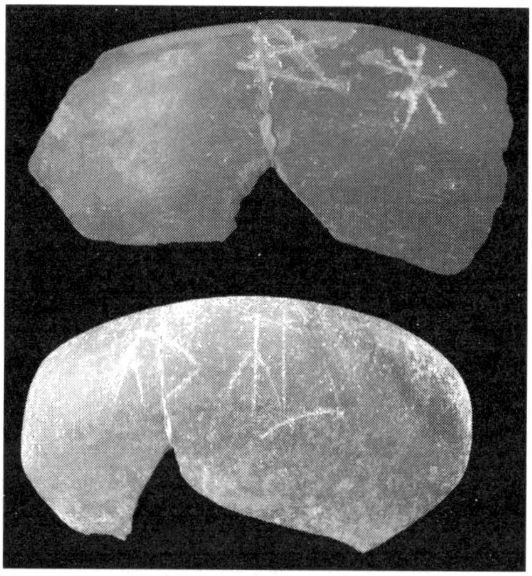

Fig. 1.9 Graffiti marks on potsherds.

There are about fifty almost complete post-firing signs engraved on the shoulder portion of the bowls and pots but mostly confined to the table wares of the black and red ware. Some signs are found to be compound signs consisting of more than one symbol (Fig. 1.9). A few of these occur repeatedly from different localities and levels. The more common graffiti marks are sun, *swastika*, star, ladder, *nandipada*, fish, bow and arrow, wheel, cart, etc. Few graffiti marks were found engraved at the end portion of the Brahmi inscription incised on the potsherd. Though the exact connotation of these symbols, individually or in compound form, cannot be easily guessed, but the close observation of these symbols, their places of occurrence, frequency and position clearly demonstrate that they were used to convey a certain message either pictographically or ideographically.

In case of burials, each one had a typical graffito symbol. Of the thirteen burials excavated, only three, viz., Meg. 4, 6 and 11 did not yield any graffiti on their pottery. But this may be due to the fragmentary nature of their pottery. The fact that each megalith had a special symbol engraved invariably on all its pottery may suggest that a particular symbol was somewhat important for, and closely related to, the person in whose memory that megalith was erected. As one symbol is found common to more than one burial, it may also be suggested that it is something like a clan symbol. However, this inference only goes to the symbols found in burials only. In addition to clan symbol, many more symbols have been noted in the habitation but their significance is yet to be satisfactorily explained.

BRAHMI

More than 100 potsherds bearing Brahmi letters were recovered from Period I. One burial (Meg.III) yielded a solitary sherd with Brahmi word

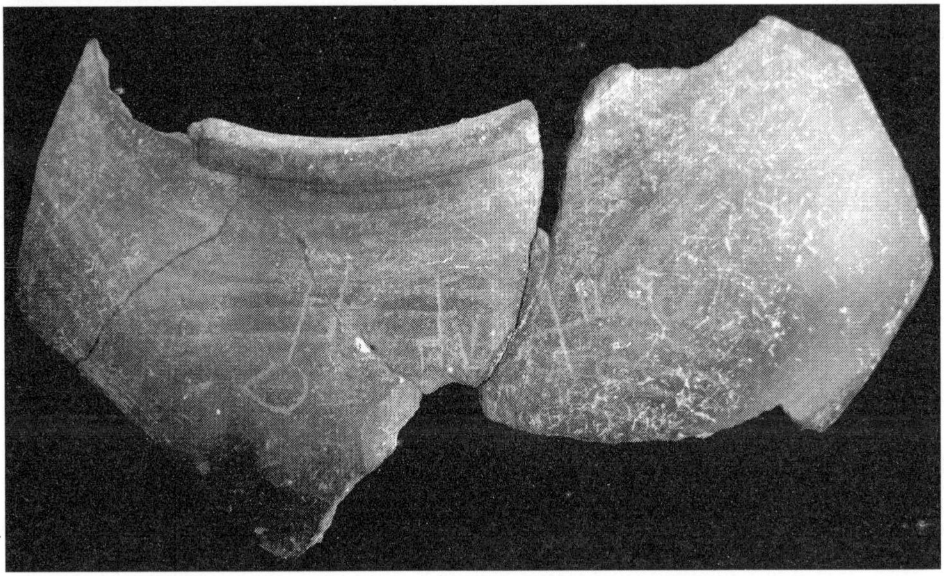

Fig. 1.10 Tamil-Brahmi inscribed potsherds reading *Visaki*.

Visaki but it seems to have been brought from the habitation site as it had already been worn out by use. The language of the inscribed potsherds is Tamil, so it has been labelled as Tamil-Brahmi. Besides the proper names like *Kannan Atan, Campan, Pannan, Antavan Atan, Atan,* etc., North Indian names like *Varuni, Kuviran, Visaki* (Fig. 1.10), *nikama,* etc. are also found. The occurrence of having affinity with North India and Sri Lanka clearly established close links with other parts of India and abroad.

PUNCH-MARKED COINS

The trenches laid on the central part of the mound yielded a silver punch-marked coin in a well stratified layer at the depth of 68 cm (Fig. 1.11). Besides this, one more punch-marked coin was collected from the surface.

BURIAL COMPLEX

The burial complex consists of more than 150 burials scattered over an area of 100 acres on the east and north-east sides of the habitation. Two types of cairn circles, consisting of either a single or double circle, were encountered. In the first type, the outer circle is made of vertical slabs planted at regular intervals and the inner circle is made of boulders. In the second type, while the outer circle is similar to the above, the inner circle is made of triangular flat stones placed in five to eight courses so as to form perfect circles. Generally, the vertical slabs of the outer circle are planted 30-50 cm below the ground level and raised 50-100 cm above it. In a few cases (Meg.II, III and VII), these vertical slabs of more than 5 m in height resemble a menhir.

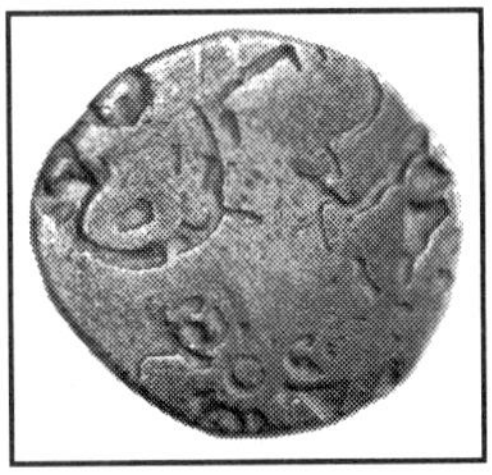

Fig. 1.11 Silver punch-marked coin.

CISTS

All the cairn circles invariably had a cist completely embedded into the soil. There are three types of cists. The first type had a simple cist with passage on the east. The second one had a transepted cist either with double or triple chambers and all the chambers were connected by portholes. The last variety had a main transepted cist flanked by two subsidiary cists. All the three cists met with a common passage at the front. All the cists were oriented in east-west direction with passage on the east. The trapeze-shaped porthole is noticed in all the three types. Interestingly, the base slab of the cist was partially broken on the north-western corner. The cists were covered by individual capstones. Some buttresses made of boulders are erected at regular intervals around the cist in the gap between the orthostats and the pit wall.

PORTHOLES

Trapeze-shaped portholes were scooped out almost at the centre of the eastern orthostats. In the case of multiple cists, the frontal slab of the main transepted cist had a porthole against each chamber as well as on the subsidiary cists. In the transepted variety, one porthole is found against the chamber facing the passage and another on the transept slab connecting both the chambers. All the portholes are trapeze in shape except one on the subsidiary cist erected on the northern side which had an arrow-head shape. The arrow-shaped porthole was closed on the outer side by a rectangular stone. Quite interestingly, in one case, i.e., Meg.II, the porthole was seen on the closing frontal slab of the passage. It seems while erecting the cist, the frontal slab might have broken completely and lost the porthole as the evidence goes, and it led the people to scoop out a fresh porthole on the frontal slab of the passage.

GRAVE GOODS

Grave goods were placed inside the cist in the passage, and also all around the cist in the gap between the cist and the inner circle of the burial. The grave goods are found against the porthole both in the passage and the cist and on the floor slab of the cist. In the case of multiple cists, one sword is invariably placed against the porthole in the passage. Chronologically, in earlier megaliths, the offerings were made inside the cist while in later ones, they were performed outside the cist. Almost all the grave goods, especially pottery, iron objects and beads, were made especially for the occasion. Invariably, all the burials yielded etched carnelian beads and a few beads of banded agate varying from a few to thousands. As stated earlier, more than 2000 carnelian beads were collected from a single burial (Meg.V).

COPPER, SILVER AND GOLD OBJECTS

In addition to the carnelian beads, copper objects like tiger figurine inlaid with alternating triangular pieces of carnelian and sapphire, spoon, bowls, stainer, bangles, etc. were found. Silver spiral bangles and rings were collected from two burials. These rings were also found interlaced with plain, barrel-shaped carnelian beads to form a necklace. Beads, rings and spiral rings made of gold were also recovered. One gold ring was made of copper wire concealed with gold foil.

IRON OBJECTS

Iron objects were collected and placed as offering in the cist, passage and outside the cist. The majority of iron objects were long and short swords, arrowheads of tanged and barbed variety, leaf-shaped arrowheads, bow, etc. Quite interestingly, horse bits and stirrups were also collected (Meg. VIII, X and XI). One unidentified object may be a horse ornament but a similar piece has been called as battle axe in earlier archaeological records. It seems to be a convention to place a sword in front of the passage. A bunch of arrowheads was placed inside the subsidiary cist against the porthole.

In addition to the antiquities, the burial yielded black and red ware, black polished ware in large quantity and red polished ware and red ware in smaller quantities. A few worn-out russet-coated ware found in burials must have been brought from the habitation. Each burial had distinct graffiti marks engraved invariably on all its pottery. The black and red ware is restricted to bowls, plates and miniature pots, whereas lids and ring-stands are made of black polished ware. Storage jars and big pots were made of red ware.

DISPOSAL OF THE DEAD

The site yielded two different modes of burials. Period I yielded disarticulate secondary burial placed on the base slab of the cist whereas Period II yielded articulated pit burials found in the habitation near the floor levels. For instance, in Meg.X the skeletal remains were secondary in nature. They were placed in a disarticulate form. Seemingly, there was no orientation. It seems that the bones were collected and placed almost at the centre of the chamber. This burial consisted of skeletal remains of two individuals, an adult and a child. The skull of the adult was kept a little away from the centre of the chamber. The humerus, pelvis, femur, tibia, fibula, ribs and part of vertebrae lay on the western side. The other skull was broken into two pieces. The tuber frontale was noticed near the pelvis portion of the adult and the occipital bone was found on the northern side adjacent to the northern orthostat. Both the skulls were facing upward. The skeletal remains could not be recovered fully as the bones were very fragile and fragmentary due to the nature of the soil and the thick deposit covering them.

Interestingly, these skeletal remains were placed on three iron swords placed in east-west orientation with tip on the west and hilt on the east. The first sword was placed on the northern side but adjacent to the skull of an adult. The second one was behind the skull of a child and the third one was found opposite the second one but on the southern side of the skeletal remains. One small unidentified iron object, probably a ring, was collected near the leg portion of the adult.

Besides, more than 500 globe-shaped etched carnelian beads were collected. Below the adult skull was found a gold spiral. The carnelian beads placed just below the skull seem to have formed a necklace intercepted by gold beads. A copper stud probably used by the adult was also recovered. In the north-west corner of the chamber was found a small pot of red ware having straight-sided neck with broad shoulder and conical base. Just 20 cm above the skeletal remains, two identical conical vases of black-and-red ware were placed on either side of two black and red ware bowls and a globular pot of red slipped ware.

Three pit burials belonging to Period II were unearthed. In the first burial, an adult male was buried in the *padmasana* posture. He was wearing a copper ring in the right hand finger. In a second burial, a child was found buried in a crouched position. The third multiple burial, probably a father, mother and a child, were rested in a pit dug into the natural soil.[2] At Kodumanal, they buried their dead in east-west orientation with head facing upward. In Period I, they were disarticulate secondary burials buried in the cemetery located away from the habitation. In Period II, they were articulated and primary burial was found within the habitation. The grave goods are totally absent in Period II.

HABITATION AND GRAVES

The occurrence of graffiti marks, Brahmi letters, russet-coated ware, carnelian and agate beads, iron objects like swords and arrowheads, the east-west orientation of the skeletal remains, pottery types like ring-stands, plates and bowls, iron slag found mixed with cairns both in the habitation and burial clearly establish the relation between the habitation and the burial. The pottery placed in the burials is made for the occasion and is purely ritualistic in nature. The grave goods were all placed as single time deposit and do not have any daily usage value. Naturally, therefore, the pottery from graves are qualitatively inferior to the ones found in the habitation. Otherwise, the amount of data collected both from the graves and burials clearly indicate that the people living in the nearby habitation in fact constructed these burials for their dead.

From the evidence collected from the site, it is obvious that Kodumanal chronologically coincides with the description found in Sangam anthologies and particularly with the poem *Patiruppattu* (Poem 67 and 74), which defines this site as a bead-making centre. The palaeography of Brahmi letters engraved on the potsherds and the proper names they represent are similar to the names of persons found in the Sangam literature. Some names like *Kannan, Sattantai,* etc. clearly indicate clans that exist even today.

These names also link Kodumanal to the Brahmi cave inscriptions of of Tamil Nadu. These also fall within the same time bracket on palaeographical grounds. The occurrence of North Indian names such as *Kuviran* and *Varuni,* and punch-marked coins indicate that the Kodumanal inhabitants as part of their inland would have obtained their carnelian from Gujarat and lapis lazuli from Afghanistan probably in exchange for beryl and quartz. Besides the occurrence of rouletted ware, a Roman coin and a terracotta figurine resembling Roman soldier collected from the surface at this site and the large quantity of Roman coin hoards discovered in this region, along the trade route connecting Musiri with Karur through Kodumanal, support the hypothesis that Kodumanal actively participated in long distance sea trade via the west coast.

The study of the fifteen human skeletal remains collected from the site, both from the graves and habitation, would throw much light on various aspects of human life.

HUMAN SKELETAL REMAINS

Of the human skeletal evidence recovered from the site of Kodumanal, remains belonging to three individuals found in the 1985 field season, one child and two adults (Specimen No. 1, 2 and 3), were studied by V. Rami Reddy and B.K. Chandrasekhar Reddy. Their research findings, primarily focussed on the morphometric analysis of cranium, were published in 1987 (Reddy and Reddy 1987). The present study deals with the entire human skeletal collection recovered during the course of excavations.

The first author undertook the laboratory study on the Kodumanal human skeletal series in 2001-2002, in the anthropology laboratory of Deccan College Post-Graduate and Research Institute, Pune, under the overall supervision of the third author. The skeletal material was sent to Deccan College in two batches. The first lot containing material from Meg. IV, IX, and X, was received in 1989, and the second lot, containing collection from Meg. V and trenches ZJ 26, in 2002. The three individuals studied by Reddy and Reddy (1987) were re-examined by the first author in Thanjavur in December 2002.

NOTES AND REFERENCES

1. Based on the comparative study made on the Tamil-Brahmi inscribed potsherds, the second author revised the date recently and pushed it back to 4th century BC. He also assigned the total cultural deposit as Early Historic with same cultural phases (Rajan 2008).
2. The skull specimens as well as the post-cranial skeletons of three individuals belonging to the third pit burial were examined by Reddy and Reddy (1987). The three individuals are determined as male, female and child of the age 35, 30 and 6 years, respectively.

2

Archaeological Context of the Burials

Fifteen skeletal specimens have been identified from the preserved set of bones that are made available for detailed anthropological laboratory study. This inventory includes the three individuals (one adult male, one adult female and a child of around 6 years of age), who were studied and reported earlier (Reddy and Reddy 1987). Reassessment of this collection resulted in identification of the fourth individual.[1] The present study deals primarily with the skeletal remains of the remaining eleven individuals, and the fourth individual mentioned above. The three specimens studied earlier by Rami Reddy and Chandrashekhar Reddy have also been re-examined from the palaeopathological perspectives. Table 2.1 provides the list of specimens included in the present study.

Description of the archaeological context of the burials, as based on the field records, is given below. Only the basic data on each burial alone is dealt here. For details of each individual burial, refer the published articles of the second author (Rajan 1990, 1991, 1996, 1999). The most noteworthy element that needs to be emphasized here is that all the skeletal remains recovered from the megalithic tombs are elite in nature and invariably associated with large amount of grave goods, particularly valuable antiquities including hundreds of carnelian beads, iron objects, beads of agate, silver and gold ornaments. Whereas, the skeletal remains recovered from the habitation area are generally devoid of any grave goods except the one with triple skeletal remains.

During the laboratory analysis of the skeletal series, the field documentation served as the base data, which was useful to assign

Table 2.1 List of specimens included in the present study

Specimen No.	Comment
Meg. I, Sp. I	Studied by Reddy-Reddy, rechecked at Thanjavur
Meg. I, Sp. II	Studied by Reddy-Reddy, rechecked at Thanjavur
Meg. I, Sp. III-A	Studied by Reddy-Reddy, rechecked at Thanjavur
Meg. I, Sp. III-B	Additional specimen found in the Reddy-Reddy collection
Meg. IV	From the 1st lot of specimens
Meg. V	From the 2nd lot of specimens
Meg. IX-A	From the 1st lot of specimens
Meg. IX-B	From the 1st lot of specimens
Meg. X-A Meg. X-B	From the 1st lot of specimens From the 1st lot of specimens
Trench ZJ26, Sp. I	From the 2nd lot of specimens
Trench ZJ26, Sp. II	From the 2nd lot of specimens
Near Tr. ZJ26, Sp. III	From the 2nd lot of specimens
Misc.	From the 2nd lot, with doubtful archaeological association
Misc.	From the 2nd lot, with doubtful archaeological association
One specimen in the State Arch. Dept., Chennai; presumed to be from Meg. XIV	Not included in the present study

association of the skeletal elements wherever the labelling of the packets was inadequate or confusing. However, it must be noted that the identification of the 'individuals' in the skeletal collection has been entirely based on the morphometric assessment of the elements.

The excavation during the initial seasons was primarily aimed to find out the chronology and cultural sequence of the site and to understand the nature of relation between the habitation and burial sites. During the first season's work, besides the two trenches on the habitation mound, three circles were opened, Meg. 1 in the habitation area, and by two cairn circles, Meg. II and Meg. III, in the cemetery area.

Meg. I was meant to expose what looked superficially like a cairn circle raised over the habitation deposits. This, however, did not contain any burial. Hence, another small trench (named during the excavation as

Fig. 2.1 Meg. I: Skeletal remains *in situ.*

Meg. I(X), was taken close to the cairn circle, which revealed the evidence of a composite pit-burial made by the first inhabitants of the locality at a depth of about 1.5 meters from the top level of the mound. This burial of post-excarnation type yielded the human skeletal remains belonging to three individuals (Fig. 2.1). All the bones were jumbled together. Some black and red ware bowls with graffiti mark were placed by the side of the skull, which was oriented to the east. Besides the pottery, there is hardly any appreciable antiquity. These three 'individuals' were studied and reported earlier by the scholars mentioned above (Reddy and Reddy 1987). Though the field records note Meg. I(X) as a separate trench, the excavator, second author of this report, to avoid possible confusion offers further clarification.[2] In the final excavation report, the excavator prefers to consider it part of the habitation. The skeletal remains from these trenches apparently did not survive to reach the laboratory. However, in the collection studied by Reddy and Reddy (1987), besides the three 'individuals' reported by them, yet another individual has been identified by the first author during her re-study of this collection. Exact archaeological context of this partially represented individual is not known. Probably, it represents either the recovery from Meg. II or Meg. III, or the fourth individual from Meg. I itself (the one excavated in the habitation), or, as stated earlier, just a mix-up of the bones in the laboratory. In the present report, this individual has been designated as 'Meg. I, Sp. III-B', and the specimen 'Meg. I Sp. III' of Reddy and Reddy (1987) has been re-designated as 'Meg. I, Sp. III-A'.

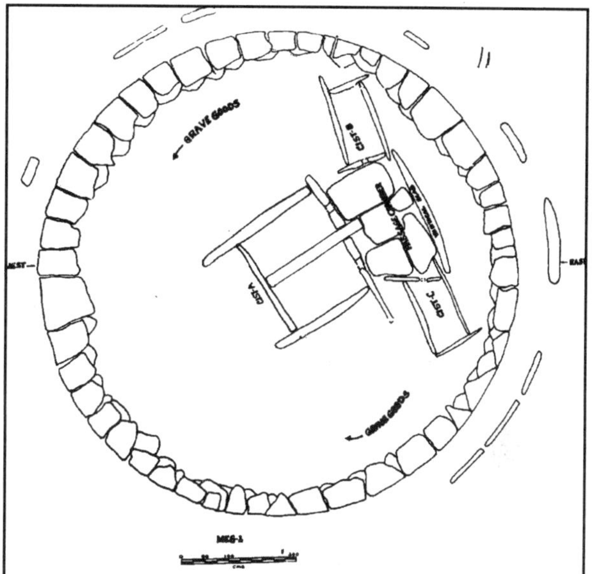

Ground plan of the Megalith 2

Fig. 2.2 Meg. II: Plan of the grave.

Meg. II is a cairn circle entombing east facing main transepted cist with two subsidiary cists (Fig. 2.2). The main transepted cist (Cist A) is constructed at the centre of the circle and two subsidiary cists at the front on either side of cist A. The two subsidiary cists faced each other, and were oriented in north-south direction. The gap between the two cists served as a common passage leading to all the cists. Two menhirs were installed as part of the outer circle. The main transepted cist had trapeze-shaped porthole against two chambers and the first subsidiary cist facing south had a key-hole type porthole. The remaining north-facing subsidiary cist had a trapeze-shaped porthole. It yielded 80 carnelian beads besides usual grave goods like four-legged jars of red slipped ware, bowls, plates and pots of black and red ware, ring-stands and miniature bowls of black slipped ware and huge jars of red ware. The iron objects include arrowheads, swords, daggers and hoes. Storage jars and four-legged jars were placed in the periphery, and ring stands bowls and dishes were placed a little inside. These grave goods were placed around the main cist in the gap between the inner circle and the main cist.

Meg. III is also a cairn circle entombing east-facing transepted cist with passage. The outer circle had a menhir (Fig. 2.3). One of the important feature of this burial is that it yielded a copper tiger figurine inlaid with semi-precious stones like carnelian and sapphire alternatively on the body

Fig. 2.3 Meg. III: General view.

of the tiger. Two copper bowls and flower motif probably fixed on the bowl as finale were also recovered along with the tiger figurine. Besides, a broken piece of a russet-coated ware with inscribed Brahmi letters reading *visaki* is collected from this burial.

Meg. IV is a disturbed urn burial exposing its mouth portion on the surface. The urn was found placed in a shallow pit of 1.10 m depth. The urn is ill-fired coarse red ware having heavily rolled rim, globular body and flat bottom. Nail-impressed designs were found on the shoulders of the urn. It had 70 cm diameter at the mouth and 1.10 m diameter at the centre with a height of 1 m. A few grave goods such as ring-stands of black polished ware and miniature bowls in black and red ware were placed inside the urn. The bone relics were placed at the bottom of the urn. As indicated in the field notes, the individual interned in this burial was an infant, but the laboratory study confirms the adult status of the individual. Only a few medium-sized fragments of cranium, teeth and a piece of scapula and a vertebral fragment represent this individual. The preserved fragments are sturdy but too fragmentary, making it difficult to carry out any morphometric analysis for this individual.

Fig. 2.4 Meg. V: General view.

Meg. V is a big cairn circle but slightly smaller than Meg. II. It lies amidst a cluster of cairn circles (Fig. 2.4). The inner circle is built of triangular slabs kept one upon the other like a wall and the outer circle is built of rectangular slabs planted vertically upwards. Generally, occurrence of cist is noticed at the centre of the circle, but in this case the cist was found towards the eastern half of the circle. There was a main transepted cist (Cist A) at the centre and two subsidiary cists at the front on either side of cist A. The two subsidiary cists faced each other, and oriented in north-south direction. The gap between the two cists served as a common passage leading to all the cists. Structurally speaking, it is similar to Meg.II. A gap of 200 cm was maintained between the orthostats of cist A and the placement of the offerings. The offerings were mainly of four-legged jars of red slipped ware, bowls and dishes of black and red ware, miniature bowls and ring-stands of black polished ware, and storage jars of red ware. Storage jars and four-legged jars were placed in the periphery and ring-stands, bowls and dishes were placed a little inside. At one place, more than 10 dishes of black and red ware were found. Though the offerings were arranged in a regular manner, they were in disarray due to heavy load of the cairns above them and most of them were defaced due to crushing. On the southern side of cist A, two crossed iron bars were placed 100 cm apart. The bars were heavy measuring 136 cm in length and 5 cm in breadth and thickness. Quite near to them, on the eastern side was kept a shield-like round iron object. A sword measuring 40 cm in length, 5 cm in breadth and 2 cm in thickness was found to the northwest of cist A. It was kept vertically downward, the point piercing the soil. Another interesting object found in the same place is a copper bowl. After the offerings were made, the cairns were packed up to a height of 1.80 cm above the ground level and 65 cm above the capstone of cist A.

The floor slab in each chamber was broken intentionally at the centre. Below this, a pit was dug to a depth of 50 cm. These pits perhaps would have served as collecting pits for the water, which was poured in the course of ceremonies. A few beads were also found in these pits. Both the chambers of cist A yielded a 2.20 cm deposit mixed with *kankar* and there was a 10 cm vacant gap on the top. The offerings inside the cist were mostly found below the level of porthole. Carnelian beads, decorated bone objects, antler and iron chisels were the antiquities collected from the cist.

The subsidiary cists B and C did not yield any antiquities or important objects except a carnelian bead found at a depth of 160 cm in cist B. No cranial elements could be collected for this individual. The recovery includes just a few pieces of ribs and post-cranial long bone mid-shafts. The bone pieces were collected from cist B at a depth of 100 cm. The base of this cist reached a depth of 155 cm. In the passage also, more than 10 carnelian beads were found. Two flat stone slabs were found against the portholes. After removal of the slabs, just near the porthole of cist C, a dagger was noticed in north-west to south-east direction. One of the important discoveries of this burial is the collection of about 2220 carnelian beads from a small pit dug besides the main cist. The occurrence of 2220 carnelian beads in a single burial may be the first instance of its kind in India.

Meg. IX is relatively a small cairn circle entombing a simple cist with a passage on the east (Fig. 2.5). The cairns were made of limestone with occasional mixture of granite and few iron slags. The burial had a total diameter of 6 m and was raised 1 m above the present ground level. The east-west oriented cist was placed at a depth of 148 cm in a rectangular pit dug into the natural soil measuring 360 cm x 185 cm. The cist was built of four orthostatus and one base slab. It was covered by a capstone. The passage on the east was made up of two vertical slabs placed on the east and north, whereas on the southern side limestone slabs were placed

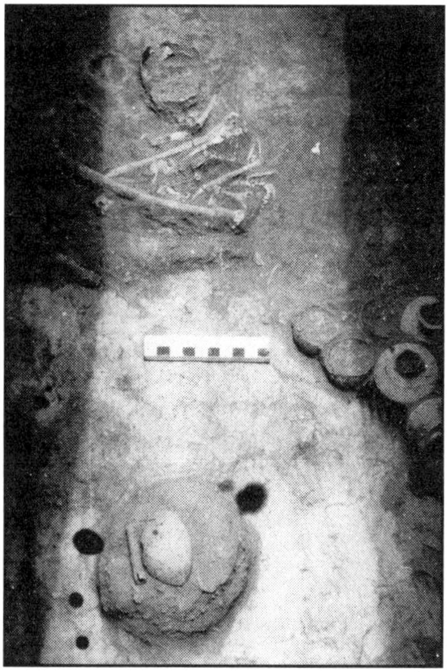

Fig. 2.5 Meg. IX: Skeletal remains *in situ.*

in courses to form a wall-like structure. A trapeze-shaped porthole was made on the eastern orthostat of the cist. A rectangular slab closed this porthole on the exterior surface. The grave goods were noticed at three places, i.e., surrounding the cist, in the passage against the porthole, and at the base of the cist.

Grave goods consisted of pottery and different types of iron objects. On the western side of the skeletal remains, near the southern orthostat, were placed four black and red ware bowls and three narrow-necked vases of red polished ware kept on the ring-stand of a black polished ware. Besides, a bowl near the northern orthostat, a narrow-necked vase and iron socket were also collected. The skeletal remains and the grave goods were completely covered with 30 cm thick deposit of soil and limestones. Above this, near the porthole, a triangular slab was placed and around this a knife, rod, arrowhead (all made of iron) and quite a number of broken potsherds were collected. There was also a barrel-shaped pendant made of iron cover with copper sheet/foil.

A secondary burial consisting of two skulls and post-cranial elements was noticed over the base slab, almost at the centre, within the cist. They were placed in disarticulated form in east-west orientation with head towards the east. One of the skulls faced west and the other skull found adjacent to this on the northern side was tilted in north-south direction. The whole skeletal remains occupied an area of about 60 sq. cm. The humerus and femur were placed cross-wise, on the western side of the skull. In between these two was put the pelvis. The mandible of the first skull was kept away from the skull on the southern end of the humerus. The radius, ulna, fibula, tibia and few ribs were piled in a rectangular space.

Fig. 2.6 Meg. X: General view.

Skull 1 (Meg. IX-B) is half broken horizontally. The parietals and frontal bone of this specimen could not be identified in the field, nor could their presence be confirmed in the laboratory. Skull 2 (Meg. IX-A) was also horizontally broken, and the palatal and frontal bones joining at the bregma were crumbled inside the skull.

As stated above, remains of two individuals were crumbled together posing lots of limitations for ascribing the skeletal elements individually. Especially, identifying elements of the thoracic cage and teeth was most problematic. Use of preservative in the field has no doubt strengthened the bones, but at the same time it puts severe limitations for morphological and pathological assessment. In this report, as stated earlier, the individuals represented here have been numbered as Meg. IX-A and IX-B. Meg. IX-A is represented by almost complete but damaged cranium and post-cranial elements, while Meg. IX-B has partially preserved cranium and few long bones from upper and lower extremity.

Meg. X is the biggest cairn circle found in the second group of burial complex near the village Siviyarpalayam (Fig. 2.6). This burial had stone boulders as its inner circle instead of wall-like structure as noticed in the other burials. The comparative study made based on the nature of antiquities, pottery and the structural elements of the burial within the burial complex indicates that it is comparatively earlier than all the burials excavated at this site.

This cairn circle measuring 11.10 m diameter entombed one main cist (cist A) and two subsidiary cists (cist B and C). Cist A is a transepted one and the rest two, cist B and C, are of a simple type. Each cist was covered by individual capstones. All the three cists had a common passage in front of them. The inner circle, as mentioned above, was made of stone boulders and the outer one was made of stone slabs planted vertically into the ground at regular intervals.

Fig. 2.7 Meg. X: Skeletal remains *in situ.*

The east-facing main cist (cist A) was further subdivided into two equal chambers. Only the northern chamber of this cist had skeletal remains at the base over the floor at a depth of 185 cm. The skeletal remains were found in association with a number of antiquities like beads made of gold and carnelian, gold spiral, iron swords and small pots. All the grave goods were confined to the central part of the chamber but quite near to the northern orthostat.

The skeletal remains were secondary in nature. They were placed in a disarticulated form. Seemingly, there was no orientation (Fig. 2.7). This burial consisted of remains of two individuals. According to excavators, one of these is an adult specimen and the other is a child, but apparently both are adult specimens. For study purpose, they are numbered as Meg. X-A and X-B. The skull of one person (X-A?) was kept little way from the centre of the chamber. The humerus, pelvis, femur, tibia, fibula, ribs and part of vertebrae lay on the western side. The other skull (X-B?) was broken into two pieces. The frontal portion of the skull was noticed near the pelvis portion, and the occipital bone was found on the northern side adjacent to the northern orthostat. Both the skulls were facing upward. The skeletal remains could not be recovered fully as the bones were too fragile and

Fig. 2.8 Trench ZJ26, Sp. I: Skeletal remains *in situ.*

fragmentary due to the nature of the soil and the thick deposit covering them.

Interestingly, these skeletal remains were placed on three iron swords placed in east-west orientation with tip on the west and hilt on the east. The first sword was placed on the northern side but adjacent to the skull of one adult (X-A). The second sword was behind the skull of X-B, while the third one was found opposite to the second one but on the southern side of the skeletal remains. One small, unidentified iron object, probably a ring, was collected near the leg portion of one skeleton (X-A?).

Besides, more than 500 globe-shaped etched carnelian beads were collected. Below one skull was found a gold spiral. The carnelian beads placed just below the skull seem to have formed a necklace intercepted by gold beads. A copper stud was also collected. In the north-west corner of the chamber was found a small pot of red ware having straight-sided neck with broad shoulder and conical base. Just 20 cm above the skeletal remains, two identical conical vases of black and red ware were placed on either side of two black and red ware bowls and a globular pot of red slipped ware.

Detailed comment on sex identification of these specimens appear later in the report, but it would be interesting to note that the specimen named as X-A is male, while the other one (X-B), identified as a child in the field, is in fact an adult female.

The skeletal remains coming from this burial are fragmentary in nature. Not a single long bone from any of these individuals is complete. Meg. X-A is represented by fairly large number of bones, whereas Meg. X-B is very fragmentary, and only a few bones are preserved.

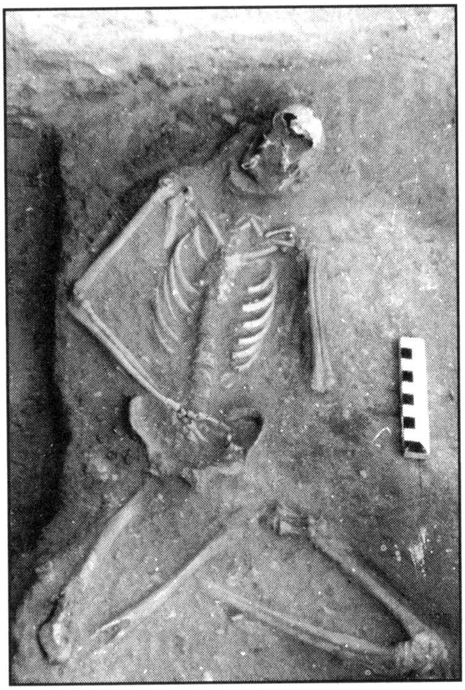

Fig. 2.9 Trench ZJ26, Sp. II: Skeletal remains *in situ*.

In addition to the skeletal remains recovered from the megalithic circles, two individuals come from the habitation levels. The excavator made cuttings at the highest point of the mound where the total deposit was about 190 cm thick. Of the four trenches dug, the trench ZJ 26, though disturbed by a huge pit, was interesting as it contained two full skeletons in its undisturbed upper levels. A pit measuring 200 x 60 cm contained two skeletons one above the other with some gap in between. The first skeleton appeared at a depth starting from 35 cm and ending in 65 cm. Some 15 cm below was found the second skeleton. The first skeleton with all the bones and the skull belonging to a child was oriented east to west, the head being on the east facing north. It is placed in a crunched position (Fig. 2.8). Actually it was kept lying on its right side so that it faced the north. It was a fully articulated skeleton but kept in a crouched position it measured only 60 cm lengthwise. The skull was in a good state of preservation but the ribs and pelvis were mutilated to some extent. The second skeleton belonged to an adult. It was again a fully articulated skeleton and was oriented east to west, the head on the east and facing above. The body was kept so as to form a *padmasana* posture, the legs being folded and the right leg being placed on the left one (Fig. 2.9). The folded right hand was on pelvis and the left hand palm was touching the mandible. The skeleton measured 118 cm lengthwise and 77 cm breadthwise. There was another skull at a depth of 60 cm a little to the south of the skeletons. Perhaps this was also part of a full skeleton and the cutting of the huge pit had displaced it out of its context. The two specimens from this cutting have been described as Sp. I and Sp. II. In addition, a third individual has been identified from the same collection, which is labelled as Sp. III.

Other than these skeletal elements described above, there are a few bones, presumably belonging to two separate individuals, the archaeological association of which cannot be established. These sets of bones have been described as 'miscellaneous collection' and numbered as misc. 1 and misc. 2. These bones were found while sorting the bones from trench ZJ26, specimen I and III. The archaeological context of these remains is uncertain and they are described here under the presumption that they are from the Kodumanal collection.

Though not included in the present study, it is worth mentioning that one additional specimen collected from Meg.XIV from subsequent Kodumanal excavations is presently kept at the Tamil Nadu State Department of Archaeology, Chennai. The second author excavated this burial as a part of joint project with the Tamil Nadu State Archaeology Department. The full report of the excavation has been published by the second author (Rajan 1999).

The above information clearly provides the cultural context in which these skeletons were recovered. There are two sets of skeletal material, one from the pit burial of the habitation and another from the chamber tombs of the megalithic grave. The skeletal remains recovered from habitation are devoid of much grave goods particularly of the luxury items or one may say they were simple in nature. The second set of skeletal remains recovered from chamber tombs met with rich grave goods and elite in nature. These two types of graves, in addition to the one found in urn burial, suggest that there were different modes of disposal of the dead used by the different communities of Kodumanal society. Beyond these modes, there is also possibility of cremation. By keeping all these limitations and complexities, the anthropological studies have been made. Results of anthropological investigations are discussed in the present report.

NOTES AND REFERENCES

1. The fourth individual probably is a mix-up that happened in the laboratory at Department of Archaeology and Anthropology, Tirupathi during the course of examination by Dr. Rami Reddy.

2. In the first seasons of excavation, an unusual heap of stones were found in the habitation. To test this heap, an excavation is carried out and is labelled as Meg.I and with extended trench as Meg. I(X), with the assumption that it is a cairn packing (a megalithic burial). After the excavation of this heap of stones and the adjoining actual burial complex, it has been realised that these heaps are later day man-made structures. After the five seasons of excavations, the labels Meg. I and Meg. I(X) have been removed and they have been placed as a part of the habitation falling in the X-quadrant. The label Meg. I is redesignated to another burial excavated in the burial complex between Meg. II and Meg. VIII. So, the specimens studied by Dr. Rami Reddy are part of the habitation and belong to the cultural phase IB.

3

Skeletal Preservation and Inventory

Inventory of the skeletal elements available for study is given in Table 3.1. Though no individual in the Kodumanal skeletal series is represented by a complete set of bones, in general, the preservation status of the skeletal series is good. The bones are fragmentary, yet there is minimal amount of weathering. As a result, reconstruction of cranial vault is possible, at least partially, in some cases. However, except a few specimens like IX-A, most of the facial skeletal is missing for all the individuals. Dentition is preserved in fairly good condition in their respective crypts. Long bone diaphyses are better preserved but the extremities are broken, and at least in some cases the loss is very recent, either during the excavation process or transportation. Thoracic cage is the least preserved portion in most of the specimens. The field documentation very much indicates presence of these elements, but no meaningful traces of these elements are noticed in the packets received in the laboratory. Apparently, they were too fragile to be lifted.

The other main problem faced while sorting the specimens in the laboratory is of mixing of bones. There seems to be a severe problem of mix-up in the trunk containing skeletal remains from Meg. I. The earlier scholars, while sorting the material in 1987, mention only three specimens in their assemblage. Even the excavator mentions only three individuals from this grave pit. However, while reopening the trunk in December 2002 at Kodumanal, one additional specimen was found. Though this fourth specimen is not fully represented, certainly the inventory includes

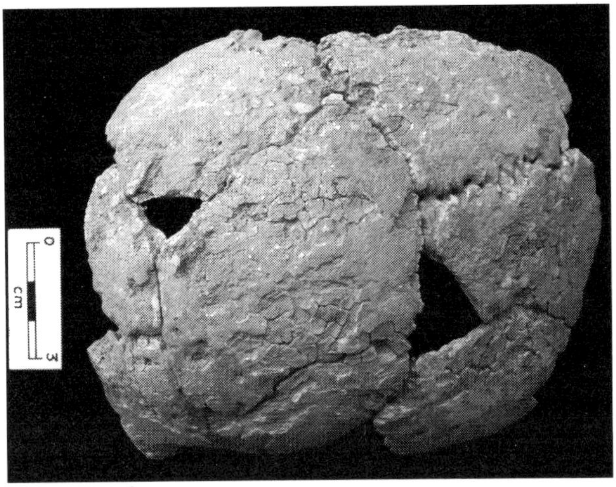

Fig. 3.1 Sp. IV: Cranium, *norma verticalis.*

some long bones and a mandible, which do not go with the specimens described earlier. This assemblage represents a young child. The association of these skeletal elements cannot be confirmed in the laboratory. Apparently, as mentioned earlier, it might be representing a ill-represented individual from Meg. II or Meg. III.

The mandible and facial skeleton of Meg. I, Sp. II (female) was reported with photographs in 1987 publication. The jaw bone is found missing in the collection now. Although most of the bones of Meg. I, Sp. I and Meg. I, Sp. II were labelled while repacking, some bones do not have any label and the bags used for packing are torn. As a result, many long bones were mixed up; during the present study, this assemblage has been sorted out to the best possible extent. Also needs to be mentioned that there are three bags containing small bone fragments belonging to long bones, cranium and other parts of the body, which could not be associated with any of the specimens in the absence of labels.

There were two bags labelled as Meg. V and Meg. 6 (Meg. VI?) in the collection. However, in archaeological field notes for Meg. VI, there is no reference about any bone findings. Moreover, some bone fragments from bag labelled as Meg. 6 articulate perfectly with the bones coming from the bag of Meg. V. Based on these criteria and also overall morphological similarity of bones coming from these two bags, the material is considered to be of a single individual. There is an extra femoral fragment in this collection. The archaeological or anatomical context of this bone remains unknown. There are some non-human bones as well in this collection. Considering all these limitations, the description on Meg. V is to be read with caution.

Table 3.1 Preservation and Skeletal Inventory

Sp. No.	Skull	Thoracic region	Upper extremity	Lower extremity
Meg. IV (Fig. 3.1)	Fifteen cranial fragments including almost complete frontal portion and partially preserved RL parietals, articulated. Occipital fragment, which could not be articulated with other bones. From the facial region, fragments of RL orbital roof, two fragments of RL maxilla, and R side mandibular fragment. Maxilla: R side fragment holding RC, RPm1, RPm2, RM1, RM2, RM3; another piece holding LI1, LI2 and LC. Mandible: R side fragment with RC, RPm1, RPm2, RM2 and RM3 *in situ*. Two isolated teeth: LM1 and LM2.	One broken thoracic vertebra.	Scapula: R side fragment with broken glenoid cavity, coracoid and acromion processes.	Nil
Meg. V	No bones from cranial and facial part. Only two isolated broken teeth from Maxilla: LI1 and RM2	10 small-sized rib fragments.	Scapula: RL fragment of coracoid process. Several long bone fragments, some of them are of humerus. One broken metacarpal and 3 phalanges.	Femur: R (?) mid-shaft portion, L damaged distal extremity with both broken condyle. Patella: small fragment, side uncertain.

Table 3.1 *contd.*

Sp. No.	Skull	Thoracic region	Upper extremity	Lower extremity
Meg. V contd.				Tibia: R proximal side severely damaged. Fibula: R 3/4th shaft fragment, L small shaft fragment. There are two bone fragments probably belonging to tarsal region. Metatarsal: one proximal part of 1st, side uncertain and R 5th one.
Meg. IX-A (see Figs. 4.1 to 4.5)	Almost complete articulated cranium, except L frontal, L parietal, part of L zygomatic arch. Almost complete *norma basalis*. Few cranial fragments probably coming from the parietal region. Complete facial skeleton. Maxilla: Complete bones with empty sockets of RLI1, RLI2, and RLC; rest of the teeth (RLPm1, RPm2, RLM1, RLM2 and RLM3) *in situ*. RC found isolated. LPm2 missing.	Atlas: R half, Axis: fragment of dens epistropheus. 28 vertebral and 90 rib small-/ medium-sized fragments belonging to Meg. IX-A and IX-B. The exact individual ascription of these pieces is not possible.	Clavicle: R almost complete but damaged at both extremities. Scapula: RL represented by acromion process. (There are 3 pieces of axillary border, exact association of which – Meg. IX-A or IX-B – is not known.) Humerus: R complete shaft without proximal end and laterally damaged distal extremity; L partially preserved in two fragments.	Femur: R complete shaft with damaged head, lesser and greater tronchanter, and broken distal extremity; L complete shaft with part of neck and missing lesser tronchanter, distal extremity. Tibia: RL complete shafts with partially preserved distal extremities, L side bone damaged severely and glued together in field.

Table 3.1 *contd.*

Sp. No.	Skull	Thoracic region	Upper extremity	Lower extremity
Meg. IX-A contd.	Mandible: Complete mandible except R coronoid process. Crowns of all anterior teeth (RLI1, RLI2, RLC, LPm1 and LPm2), are lost. Rest of the teeth (RPm1, RPm2, RLM1, RLM2 and RLM3) *in situ*.		One is 8 cm long mid-shaft portion and another is damaged distal extremity. Radius: RL shaft fragments Ulna: R 3/4th from proximal side, 1/4th distal part missing; L complete shaft with both extremities missing. Six damaged metacarpals, uncertain identification.	Fibula: R more than half from distal side; L distal half shaft, with broken extremity. One broken meta-tarsal with uncertain identification. There are approximately 14 bone fragments, which can be tentatively identified as tarsals and 16 phalanges probably belonging to two individuals (Meg. IX-A and IX-B).
Meg. IX-B (Figs. 3.2 to 3.5)	Almost complete cranial cap; frontal with damaged R side, RL parietals, occipital damaged on R side, L side foramen magnum with occipital condyle, part of zygomatic arch; From the basal aspect, R petrous portion with glenoid cavity, L petrous portion and another fragment of glenoid cavity with part of sphenoid; From the facial skeleton only R side maxillary fragment with 3 teeth.	Atlas: L half with broken inferior articular surface. Axis: part of Dens epistrophei.	Clavicle: RL pieces of lateral ends. Scapula: R glenoid cavity, parts of acromion process and axillary border; L glenoid cavity, coracoid process, partially preserved axillary border and small part of acromion process. Humerus: RL complete shafts without proximal and distal extremities.	Pelvis: R part of illium with partially preserved greater sciatic notch and acetabulum, one medium-sized fragment of pelvic blade, side uncertain. Femur: R almost half damaged proximal side with missing head. Tibia: L proximal damaged cap.

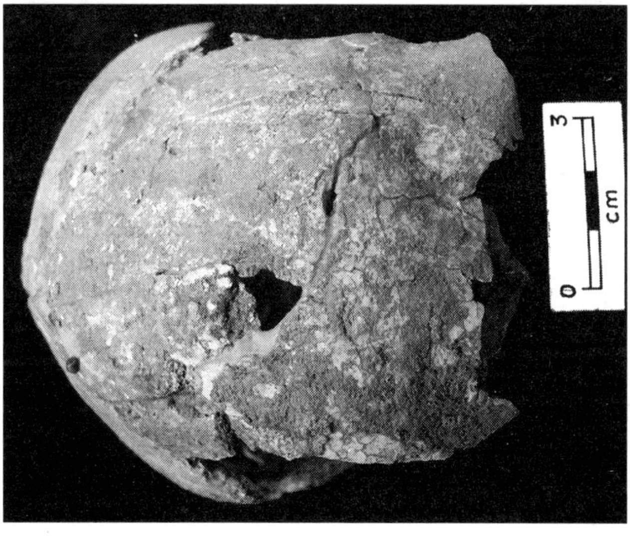

Fig. 3.2 Sp. IX-B: Cranium, *norma frontalis.*

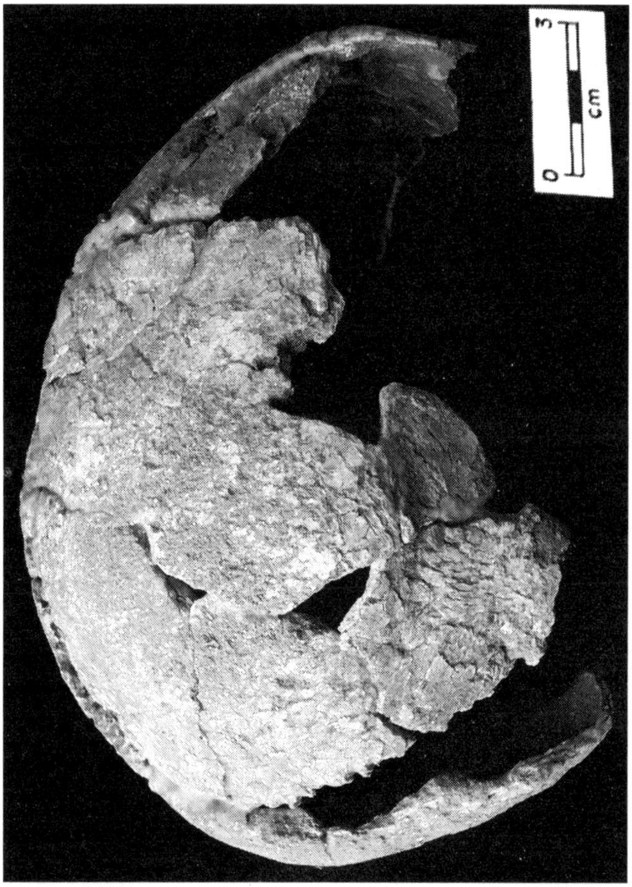

Fig. 3.3 Sp. IX-B: Cranium, *norma lateralis* (R).

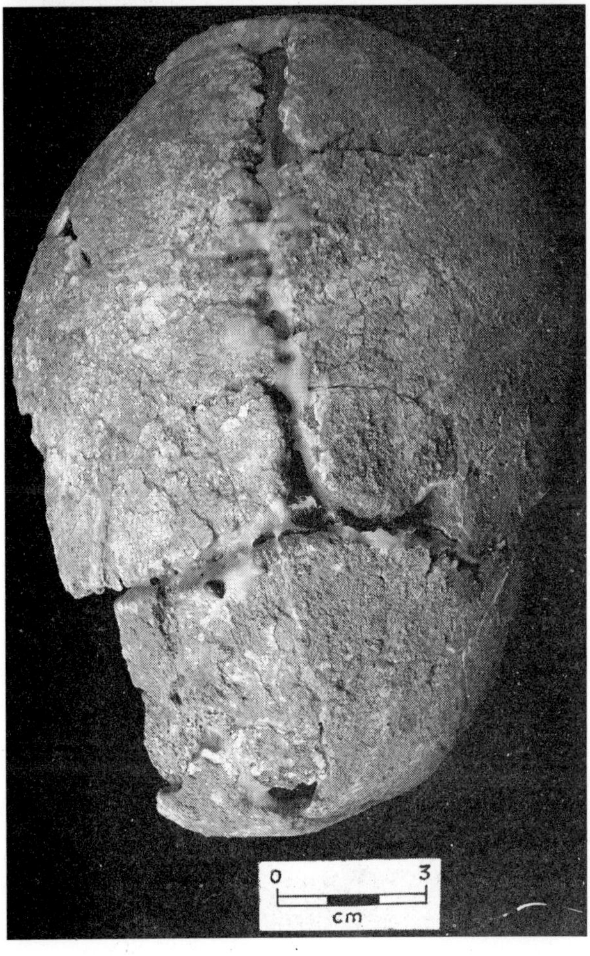

Fig. 3.4 Sp. IX-B: Cranium, *norma verticalis.*

Fig. 3.5 Sp. IX-B: Cranium, *norma occipitalis.*

Table 3.1 *contd.*

Sp. No.	Skull	Thoracic region	Upper extremity	Lower extremity
Meg. IX-B contd.	Also 17 small-sized unidentifiable cranial fragments. Maxilla: RLI1, RLI2 (isolated), RLPm1, LPm2, RLM1 and RLM2 and RM3(?). Mandible: damaged but complete mandible except broken L condyle. RI2 (isolated), RC, RPm1, RPm2, RLM1 and RM2 are *in situ*.		Radius: R proximal 3/4th with 1/4th distal side missing; L almost complete except distal extremity missing. Ulna: R (preserved in two fragments) and L almost complete except olecranon process and distal end missing.	Fibula: L (?) distal 3/4th preserved in two fragments. A small shaft fragment connecting these two fragments is missing.
Meg. X-A	Frontal: almost complete with RL orbital roof; Parietal: R partially preserved, L almost complete; Temporal: L petrous portion, L fragment of glenoid cavity, small fragment of mastoid process, side uncertain; Occipital: almost complete and basilar. Also 20 small-sized unidentifiable cranial fragments.	Nil	Clavicle: R both medial and lateral extremities but mid-shaft portion is missing, L damaged medial end; Scapula: L glenoid cavity fragment; Humerus: R medium-sized shaft fragment, medial condyle and part of trochlea from distal side, L mid-shaft fragment and broken distal end with partially preserved medial condyle and fossa;	Pelvis: there are 3 fragments probably belonging to R side. R fragment of greater sciatic notch; Femur: R proximal fragment with head, greater and lesser tronchanter; L head and neck fragment. There are 2 medium-sized shaft fragments, side uncertain; Patella: R complete;

Table 3.1 *contd.*

Sp. No.	Skull	Thoracic region	Upper extremity	Lower extremity
Meg. X-A contd.	Maxilla: all teeth are isolated. RI2, RPm1 (crown), RLPm2 (R only crown), RLM1, LM2, RM3. Mandible: L fragment holding LM1 and LM2, other teeth are isolated, RLI1, RLI2, RC, RPm1, RPm2, RLM1, RLM2.		Radius: R 1/3rd shaft fragment with tubercle, both extremities missing; L damaged proximal extremity. There are one small and another medium-sized mid-shaft fragment, side uncertain.	Tibia: R three fragments, proximal end represented by medial condyle, mid-shaft region and distal extremity; L four fragments but without articulation, both ends are damaged and 2 mid-shaft fragments; Tarsal: Talus: R half broken; L complete. There are 5 broken bones, probably damaged tarsal bones. There are 3 long bone fragments; individual identification is not possible.
Meg. X-B	30 small-medium-sized fragments, including four of the parietal region, one from occipital and two from orbital region, which includes L orbital roof. Individual identification not possible for the remaining fragments.	2 rib mid-shaft fragments.	Clavicle: L almost complete except sternal end; Scapula: R glenoid cavity; L part of acromion process; Humerus: R 3/4th distal side; L 1/4th distal fragment, extremity is missing; Radius: R almost complete shaft, both extremities lost;	Femur: two shaft fragments, sides uncertain; Tibia: R fragment of medial condyle, and from distal end part of fibular articular surface area; one mid-shaft fragment, side uncertain; Fibula: small mid-shaft fragment, side uncertain;

Table 3.1 *contd.*

Sp. No.	Skull	Thoracic region	Upper extremity	Lower extremity
Meg. X-B contd.	All teeth are isolated. Maxilla: RI1 (broken crown), RPm2, RM2, RM3 (?). Mandible: RPm1, RPm2, RLM1, LM2 and one root, unidentifiable.		L 3/4th proximal side except the head; Ulna: L 1/4th distal side and one small mid-shaft fragment, side uncertain.	Tarsal: RL talus and fragment of calcanus, side uncertain.
Trench ZJ26, Sp. I (Figs. 3.6 to 3.8)	Almost complete cranial cap, basal and facial part with some damage. Missing bones/portions are RL zygomatic arch, some small bone fragments of skull, L coronoid process and R vertical ramus. Approximately 40 small-sized cranial fragments including basal parts. Maxilla: RLdi1, Rdi2, Rdc, RLdm1, RLdm2, RLM1 and RI1, RI2, RLM2 (isolated but undeveloped) Mandible: Rdi1, Rldi2, Ldc, RLDm1, RLdm2, RLM1and RLM2 (L in crypt and R isolated)	All elements are represented. Cervical: Half broken atlas, axis, 3rd, 4th half broken, 5th, 6th and 7th in pieces. Thoracic: 3 half broken vertebrae stuck with ribs, 3 with broken bodies, 4 vertebral arches, 3 fragments of spinous process, no individual identification possible.	Scapula: R small blade fragment, L medial border with part of spine. Clavicle: L lateral half. Humerus: R complete shaft with upper margin of olecranon fossa, L complete shaft with laterally damaged distal extremity, proximal end missing. Metacarpals: R 5 with unfused 3 caps, 10 phalanges, L 3 broken, 6 phalanges.	Pelvis: R iliac fragments with partially preserved greater sciatic notch and few small-sized blade fragments. Femur: R almost complete shaft with both missing extremities, L almost complete bone damaged at greater trochanter and distal extremity. Metatarsals: 3 damaged, 3 phalanges. There are 17 damaged bone fragments probably belonging to epiphyseal caps (7) as well as tarsals (10). Individual identification not possible.

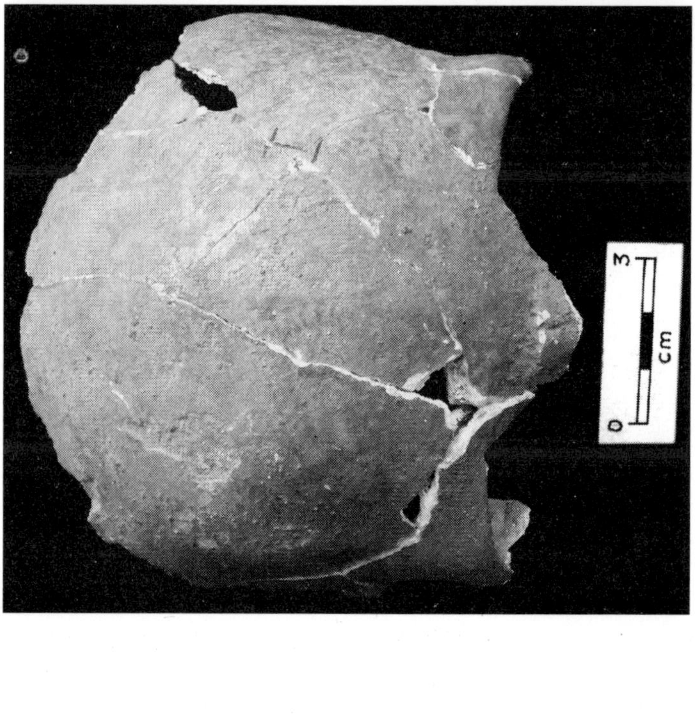

Fig. 3.6 Trench ZJ26, Sp. I: Cranium, *norma frontalis*.

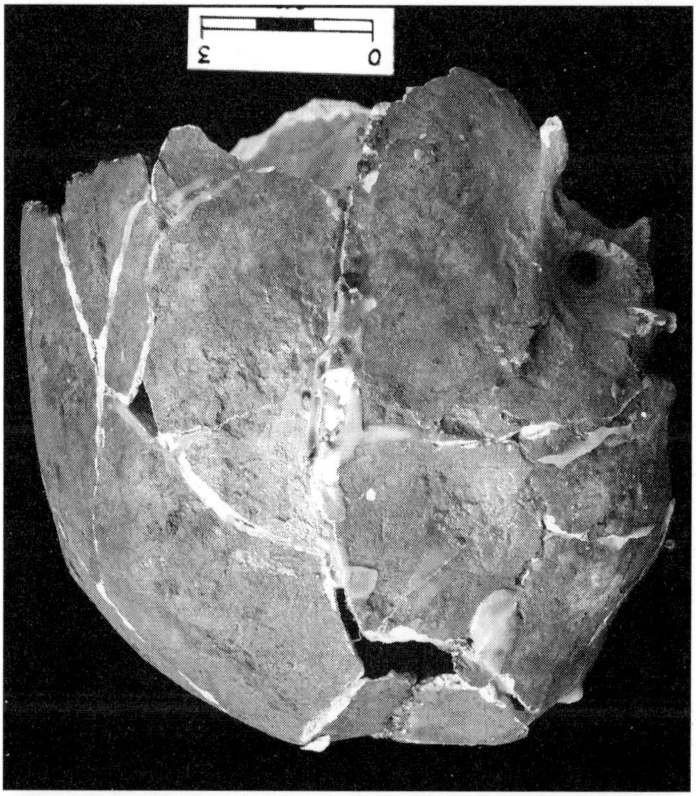

Fig. 3.7 Trench ZJ26, Sp. I: Cranium, *norma lateralis* (R).

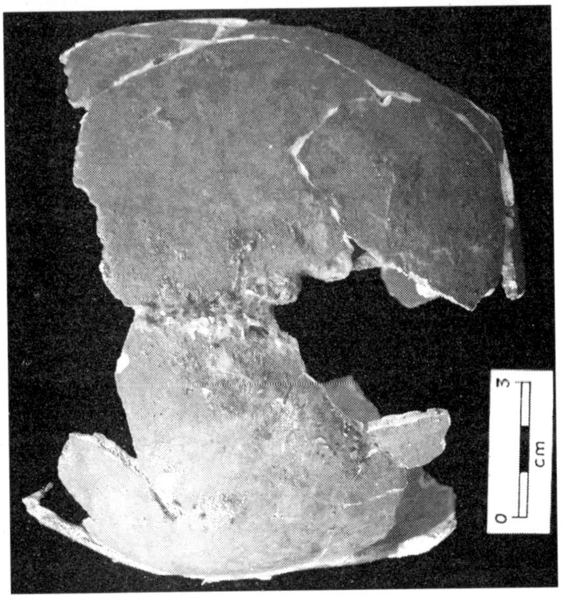

Fig. 3.8 Trench ZJ26, Sp. I: Cranium, *norma verticalis*.

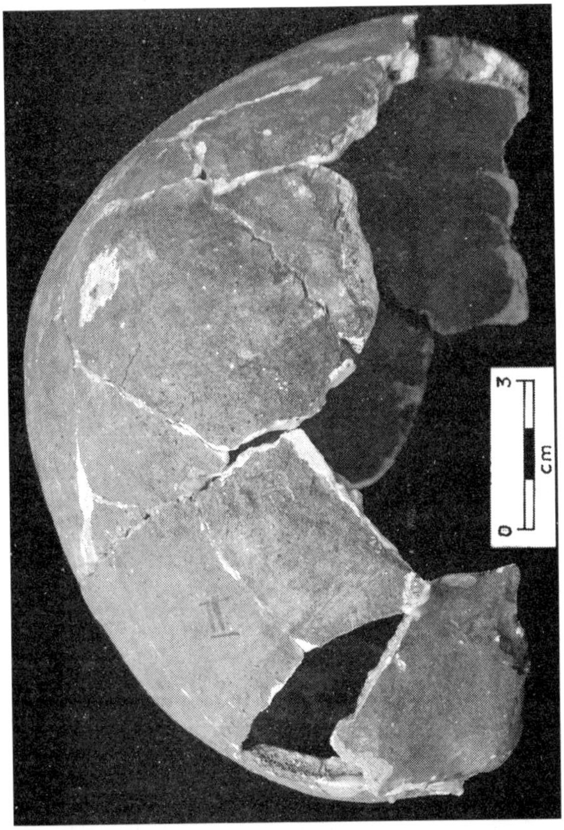

Fig. 3.9 Trench ZJ26, Sp. II: Cranium, *norma lateralis* (L).

Table 3.1 *contd.*

Sp. No.	Skull	Thoracic region	Upper extremity	Lower extremity
Trench ZJ26, Sp. I contd.		Lumber: 4 damaged vertebrae. Part of coccyx. More than 50 big-medium-small-sized fragments including sternal and vertebral ends.		
Trench ZJ26, Sp. II (Figs. 3.9 to 3.11)	Almost complete cranial cap, some parts from R parietal, RL petrous part with some portion of temporal and L orbital roof, basal portion is missing; from the facial region L zygomatic bone and small R maxillary fragment. There are 25 medium-small-sized fragments unidentified. Maxilla: R maxillary fragment holding four teeth. RI1, RI2, RC, RPm1, RLPm2, RLM1, RLM2, RLM3	Rib: approx. 50 mid-shaft, 8 sternal ends and 23 vertebral end fragments, individual identification not possible. Vertebral column: Cervical: almost complete atlas but damaged on ventral side, axis, 3 and 4th, four fragments.	Clavicle: R partially preserved in 3 fragments. One from lateral side and 2 from mid-shaft region, L almost complete with both extremities missing. Scapula: R damaged glenoid cavity, blade with spine and axillary border part of acromion process, L 3 fragments including part of spine axillary border and small part of glenoid cavity.	Pelvis: R fragment containing acetabulum, Greater sciatic notch and part of ischium, L acetabulum and part of ischium, and 2 fragments. Femur: R in 3 fragments containing shaft, head and severely damaged distal extremity, L almost complete but severely damaged proximal extremity, greater tronchanter and part of

Fig. 3.10 Trench ZJ26, Sp. II: Cranium, *norma verticalis.*

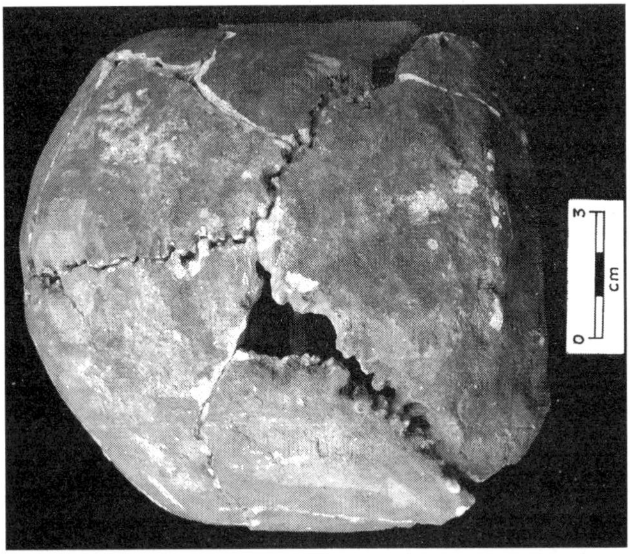

Fig. 3.11 Trench ZJ26, Sp. II: Cranium, *norma occipitalis.*

Table 3.1 *contd.*

Sp. No.	Skull	Thoracic region	Upper extremity	Lower extremity
Trench ZJ26, Sp. II contd.	Mandible: R fragment with three molars *in situ*, damaged occurred to coronoid process, L vertical ramus. RLI1, RI2, RPm1, RM1, RM2, RM3.	Thoracic: almost complete 9th (?) and 11th (?) partially damaged and 4th, 5th and 8th spinous process. Lumber: almost complete 2nd (?) and 5th (?), 2 broken bodies with superior articular surface. Sacrum and coccygeal: almost complete but partially damaged. There are 7 bodies and 15 vertebral fragments.	Humerus: R almost complete without proximal extremity but small part of humeral head fragment, L complete. Radius: RL complete (R radial cap is separated from the main bone). Ulna: RL complete (R distal part is separated from the main bone). Carpals: RL 7 bones except 4th piciform is missing from both sides. Metacarpals: RL all. Phalanges: R 14 and L 13.	lesser tronchanter missing, damage occurred to medial condyle. Patella: RL complete. Tibia: R part of proximal lateral cap, shaft and damaged distal extremity on fibular articular surface, L complete but preserved in two fragments, part of distal diaphysis broken. Fibula: R shaft with both extremities missing, L almost complete except missing distal extremity. Tarsals: RL all Metatarsals: RL all Phalanges: R 15, L 12.

Table 3.1 *contd.*

Sp. No.	Skull	Thoracic region	Upper extremity	Lower extremity
Trench ZJ26, Sp. III (Figs. 3.12 to 3.13)	Preserved elements include complete frontal, part of RL parietal, part of RL temporal, RL sphenoid, RL petrous part and mastoid process with small part of zygomatic arch, some fragments of basal part including border of foramen magnum, basilar. From facial side almost all bones are intact and articulated. Maxilla: complete but damaged and missing few teeth. LI1, LI2, RLC, LPm1 and RPm2 (in crypt), Ldm2, RLM1. Mandible: intact and sturdy. RLI1, RLI2, RLC, RLdm2, RLM1.	Two rib fragments	Clavicle: L 3/4th with sternal end. Scapula: R acromion process, L almost complete but damaged spine, caracoid and medial border. Humerus: R 3/4th shaft with both extremities missing L complete shaft with missing head and damaged distal extremity. Radius: R small mid-shaft fragment, L almost complete with some damage at distal extremity. Ulna: R almost complete with missing olecranon process, L almost complete but olecranon and distal extremity missing. One small fragment of metacarpal (?)	Tibia: R almost complete shaft with unarticulated distal cap, L almost complete shaft with both extremities missing. Fibula: L 3/4th bone from proximal side.

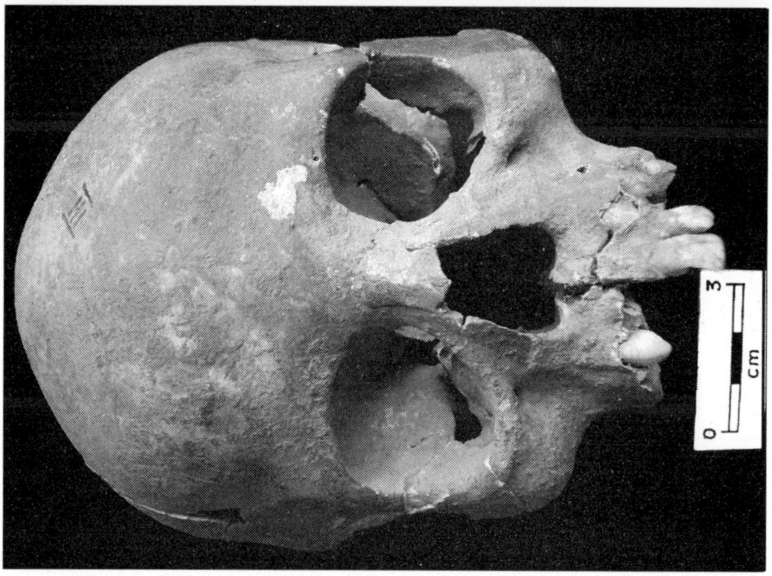

Fig. 3.12 Trench ZJ26, Sp. III: Cranium, *norma frontalis.*

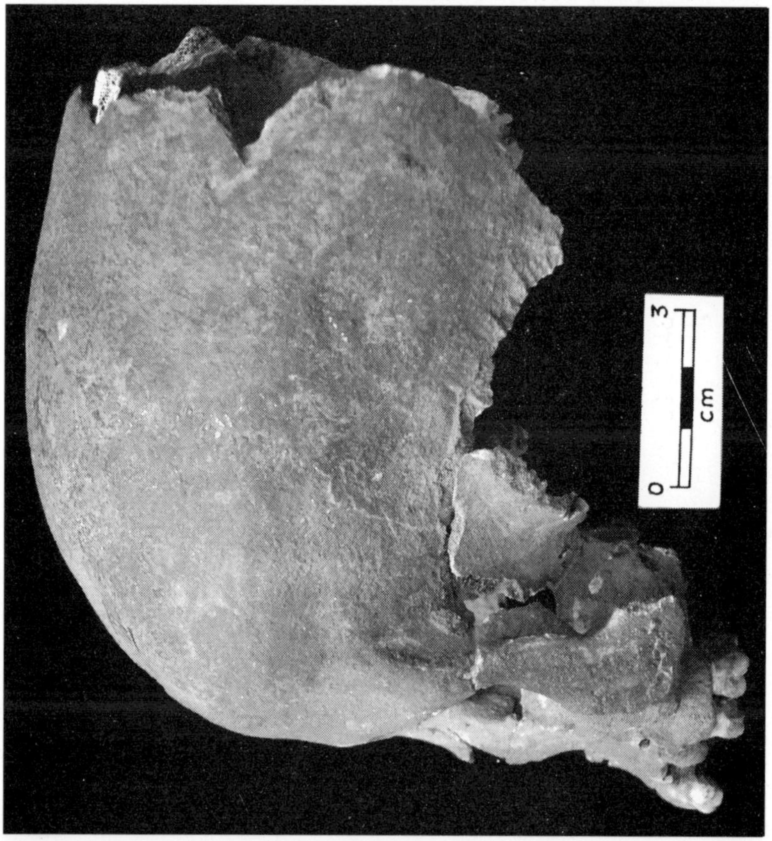

Fig. 3.13 Trench ZJ26, Sp. III: Cranium, *norma lateralis* (L).

Table 3.1 *contd.*

Sp. No.	Skull	Thoracic region	Upper extremity	Lower extremity
Skeletal series studied at Thanjavor				
Sp. I Reddy-Reddy (1987) series	Complete cranial cap including frontal, RL parietal, RL temporal with mastoid process and occipital. Missing part includes facial and basal region. Maxilla: Complete maxillary arcade. LI2, LC, RLPm1, RLPm2, RLM1, RLM2, missing teeth includes RLI1, RI2 and RC Mandible: complete mandible preserved with all teeth *in situ*. Damage only to the R condyle and RL coronoid process.	Ribs: 11 mid-shaft fragments. Vertebral column: Cervical: almost complete except R side foramina, probably 3rd one but damaged, 3 broken bodies. Thoracic: 8 damaged bodies and 3 spinous processes. Lumber: probably partially damaged 1, 2 and 5th ones, 2 damaged bodies and petal region with lost spinous process, one broken fragment of sacrum.	Scapula: axillary border, side uncertain Clavicle: L complete Humerus: R ¾ from distal side, proximal side missing Ulna: R half bone from proximal side, L ¼ proximal extremity with part of shaft Radius: R little more than ¼ from distal side, L almost complete shaft with radial tuberosity.	Pelvis: L six fragments including illac blade and part of acetabulum Femur: R more than half from proximal side, L ¾ bone with dist side missing Patella: L damaged Tibia: R 7 cm part of diaphysis from proximal side, L almost complete shaft with bone extremities missing Fibula: R 11 cm fragment of shaft from proximal side, L almost ¾ with proximal extremity Tarsals: RL damaged talus and clacanus Metatarsals: R 4 and 5, L 1 to 5 Phalanges: 6 including RL toe bone.

Table 3.1 *contd.*

Sp. No.	Skull	Thoracic region	Upper extremity	Lower extremity
Sp. II Reddy-Reddy (1987) series	Complete cranial cap including frontal, RL parietal, R temporal and occipital; from facial region L orbital margin with part of zygomatic bone, R maxillary fragment. There are some small fragments, individual identification is not possible. Maxilla: R maxillary fragment holding Pm1, Pm2, M1, M2 and M3, roots of I1, I2 and C in the jaw. Mandible: one R fragment holding only roots of RPm2 and RM1, one root fragment.	Ribs: around 30 small- and medium-sized mid-shaft fragments Vertebral column: Cervical: almost complete atlas, 3, 4 and 7 damaged bodies and 5 and 6 complete but damaged. Thoracic: 1 partially broken and 2 only body fragments Lumber: 2 half-broken part of sacrum. There are 7 vertebral fragments containing spinous process and other parts.	Clavicle: R later side with cronoid tubercle, L almost complete with both extremities missing Humerus: R complete shaft, both ends missing, L almost complete but damaged on both extremities. Radius: R almost complete with broken proximal head, L proximal extremity with radial tubercle Ulna: R ¾ from proximal side in two fragments, L almost complete haft with both extremities missing Carpals: 4, individual identification not possible	Pelvis: RL illiac fragment, 3 acetabulum and 6 small fragments, side uncertain Femur: R almost ¾ shaft with both extremities missing, L part of bone with lesser tronchanter head part side uncertain Patella: RL partially damaged Tibia: R half shaft from proximal side with out extremity L almost complete, proximal side and medial malleolus from distal extremity missing. Fibula: 2 big shaft fragment, one stuck with R radius, and other two are small, uncertain identification Tarsals: RL damaged talus, calcanus R complete but severely damaged,

Table 3.1 *contd.*

Sp. No.	Skull	Thoracic region	Upper extremity	Lower extremity
Sp. II Reddy-Reddy (1987) series contd.		There are almost 60 rib fragments of Sp. I and II mixed together.		L articular surface fragment, RL first cuniform, R small cuniform, L navicular. There are 3 tarsals with uncertain identification 6 phalanges, 16 meta tarsals-carplas with uncertain identification.
Sp. III-A Reddy-Reddy (1987) series	No bones from skullcap preserved. R mandibular fragment with Rdm1 in crypt.	28 small rib fragments.	Humerus: mid-shaft fragments, side unidentified. Radius: R distal end fragment, L almost complete Ulna: R (?) almost complete but severely damaged from both extremities.	Femur: small part of distal end, side uncertain. Fibula: mid-shaft fragment, side uncertain.
Sp. III-B Reddy-Reddy (1987) series	Almost complete cranium, but severely damaged. No bones from the facial and basal region. One tooth, probably maxillary Rdi2 is stuck with soil to humerus of Sp. II (female).	Nil	Scapula: R fragment of acromion process Radius: mid-shaft fragment, side uncertain.	Tibia: probably proximal cap fragment from lateral side.

4

Observations: Morphometry, Pathology and Demography

The anthropological observations on the Kodumanal skeletal series have been presented in four broad sections. Details of the cranial and post-cranial morphometric assessment have been provided in the first section. Important findings of the earlier work have also been enumerated while forwarding comment on the morphometric features. In the second section, observations on the dentition have been given. The skeletal and dental pathologies have been discussed in the third section. The comments on the age-sex determination appear in the fourth section.

METHODOLOGY

Morphological assessment of cranial and post-cranial bones is carried out following the *Standards* by Buikstra and Ubelaker (1994). Craniometric and osteometric methods used in this report follow Martin and Saller (1957). All the measurements, unless otherwise specified, are in millimeters. Cases where the reading is an estimated one, the measurements are recorded in bracket. Some measurements / indices are classified according to the sources quoted. Stature estimation follows the method of Trotter (1970), where racially specific equations for White populations are used.

Two basic measurements have been carried out for each tooth following the Moorrees' (1957) technique. These consist of maximum crown length (mesio-distal diameter) and maximum crown breadth (bucco-lingual diameter). Three primary comparative standards of Wolpoff (1971) in the analysis of tooth size and shape include the measure of the cross-sectional area of the tooth (CA), the ratio of MD and BL diameter (CI), and the measure of crown bulk-module (CM). Two composite figures are obtained to facilitate comparative study of dental adaptations in response to the subsistence pattern and the level of food processing technique, the total crown area (TCA), and the molar crown area (MCA). These figures are expressed in millimeters squareds (mm^2). In addition, basic data on three other indices have been provided for the maxillary and mandibular teeth. These include incisor breadth index, molarisation index and step index. The formulae used for computing these indices are as follows (Potter *et al.* 1981, Dahlberg 1963, Selmer-Olsen 1949, *quoted by* Lukacs 1985a):

Specific observations of dental morphology have been made on maxillary and mandibular deciduous and permanent teeth using reference plaster plaques prepared by the ASU Dental Anthropology System (Turner II. *et al.* 1991).

Pathological recording is based on macroscopic observations carried out using 10-X magnifying lens. All specimens having pathological lesion/ anomaly are radiographed for confirming the diagnosis taking stringent precautionary measures. Main references used while describing the pathologies and anomalies are Larsen (1997), Ortner and Putschar (1981), Roberts and Manchester (1995) and Lukacs (1989).

Sex and age determination is attempted at following the standardized criteria described in Brothwell (1981), Olivier (1969), Stewart (1979) and Buikstra and Ubelaker (1994).

A. Description of Cranial and Post-Cranial Elements

I. Cranial Elements

As stated earlier, 15 individuals comprise the Kodumanal skeletal series, of which three individuals were studied earlier (Reddy and Reddy 1987). Of the remaining 12 specimens, seven are adults and three belong to the sub-adult ages; death age of the remaining two cannot be determined with certainty. Neurocranial elements are reasonably well preserved only for six adults, while more or less complete skull with facial elements is available only for one adult individual, which form the primary subject matter of this section.

By and large there is considerable homogeneity in the skeletal series studied previously and the one being studied presently.

As stated, only one male specimen (Meg. IX-A) is in fairly good state of preservation, permitting a good assessment of cranial facial

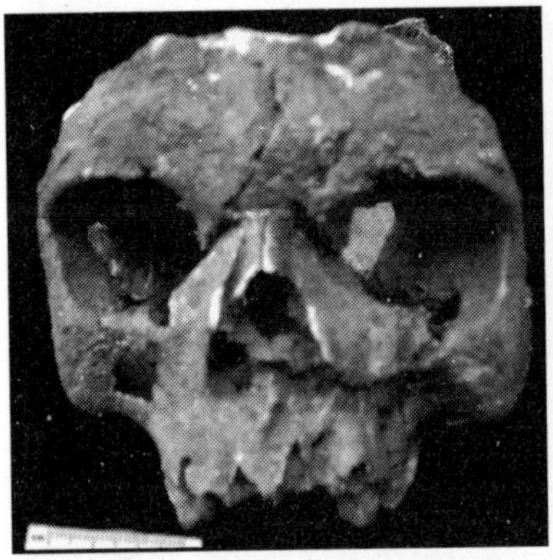

Fig. 4.1 Meg. IX-A: Cranium, *norma frontalis.*

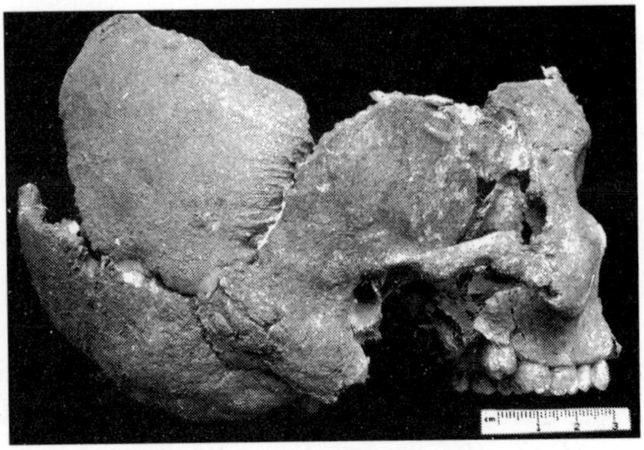

Fig. 4.2 Meg. IX-A: Cranium, *norma lateralis* (R).

morphological features (Fig. 4.1 to 4.5). Facial skeleton is not preserved for any other specimen. In the earlier series also, only one specimen, an adult female, has a fairly complete facial portion. Therefore, there are obvious limitations for forwarding a comment on phenotypic assessment of the Kodumanal population. Nevertheless, the craniometric study undertaken by Reddy and Reddy (1987) gives excellent morphometric narration of two specimens, a male and a female (Meg. I, Sp. I, and Meg. I, Sp. II). They also provide assessment of the sexual dimorphism expressed in these two specimens.

The adult male specimen (Meg. IX-A) of the present series is represented by a fairly complete skull, as stated earlier, and by post-cranial elements. The specimen is moderately built. Robusticity expressed in post-cranial elements matches the moderately built processes and tubera in the neurocranium. Temporal lines, glabellar region, parietal region and the mastoids are moderately developed. The occipital bone is rough in the nuchal region and the inion is well marked. The damage to the left parietal precludes accurate assessment of cranial breadth. However, the estimated measurement puts the skull in dolichocranial range, giving the cranial index of 72.97. Forehead is rather straight, well comparable with the Deccan Chalcolithic specimens, sloping gradually from the metopic region. Face is medium with a bizygomatic breadth of 124 mm. The face is of medium height with upper facial height of 59 mm and total facial height of 106 mm. The upper facial index is 47.58, which fails in mesen (middle upper face) category. The total facial index is 85.48 (mesoprosopic). Least frontal breadth (97 mm) when compared with maximum cranial breadth

(135 mm) gives the index of 71.85, which falls in eurymetopic category. The transverse cranio-facial index is 91.85. Face is straight (orthognathous). Palate is deep with an estimated depth of 20 mm. Orbits are horizontal and rectangular in shape. The orbital index is 89.47 (hypsichonch). Nose is broad having an index of 57.14, which falls in chamaerhinae category. Mandible is fairly built. The gnathion region is stronger than the gonial region. Ascending ramus of mandible is of medium breadth giving minimum and maximum diameter values of 32 and 33 mm, respectively.

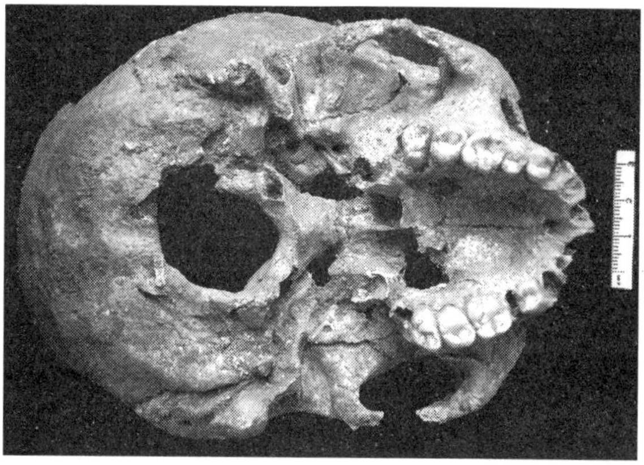

Fig. 4.3 Meg. IX-A: Cranium, *norma basalis.*

To summarise on the cranio-morphometric features of the Kodumanal series, it could be said that, in general morphological appearance the male specimens are moderately robust, the females being relatively gracile. The cranium dimensions range from mesocranial to dolichocranial category. The skull height is moderately high. The temporal lines and nuchal lines are faint but mastoids are fairly large, both in male and female specimens. Glabellar region is also prominent in most of the individuals. The forehead is vertical and gradually receding from the metopic region. The face is straight or orthognathous or slightly projecting. There is slight alveolar prognathism, however, in the specimens where facial skeleton is retained. Nose is medium but there is slight concavity evident on the nasal bones at the roots.

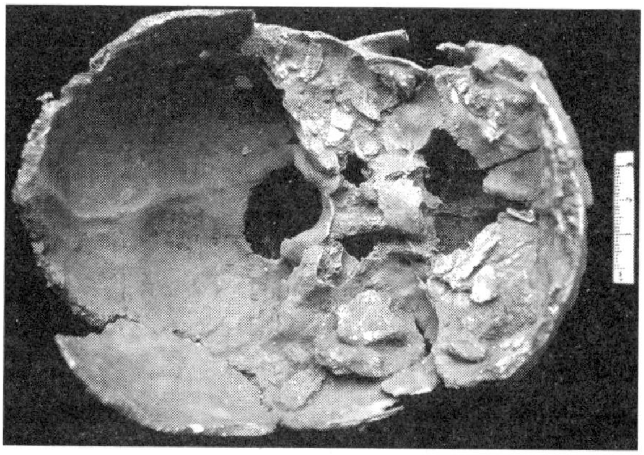

Fig. 4.4 Meg. IX-A: Cranium, *norma verticalis* exposing inner cavity.

While being aware of the *'serious limitations'* involved in comparing the Kodumanal skeletal series,

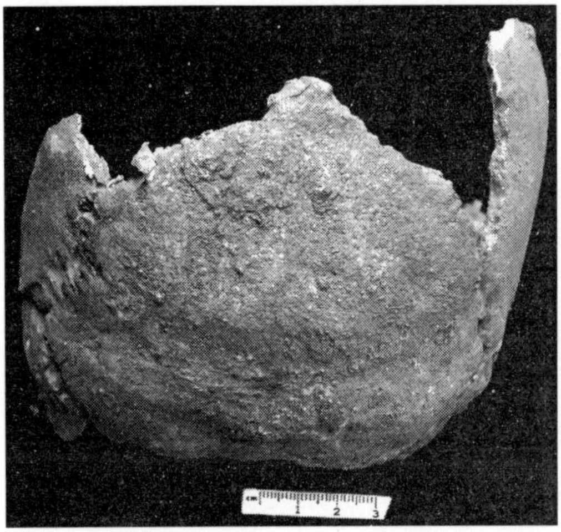

Fig. 4.5 Meg. IX-A: Cranium, *norma occipitalis.*

because of its smaller sample size and fragmentary nature of the preserved remains, with other protohistoric populations of the region, Reddy and Reddy (1987:111) attempt to evaluate the inter-population affinities. The scholars attempt to compare their sample with the Megalithic populations of Tamil Nadu, Yelleswaram (Gupta and Dutta 1962) and Adichchanallur (Chatterjee and Gupta 1963), and the Neolithic populations of Brahmagiri (Sarkar 1960), Piklihal (Ayer 1960), Tekkalakota (Malhotra 1965) and Nagarjunkonda (Gupta *et al.* 1970). They prefer to confine themselves only to these populations 'because of the fact of the location of these sites in the present Dravidian speaking states', and further comment that 'comparisons with other skeletal populations coming from the other parts of the sub-continent would become far-fetched'. On the basis of the metric data generated by them, they conclude that the specimens studied by them broadly compare with their counterparts from other sites and belong to the 'Australoid racial group'.

The present authors, however, categorically prefer not to ascribe any '*racial*' label to the population. In their opinion, one better preserved male and one female cannot be taken as '*representatives*' of the entire population.

It must be added, nevertheless, that the cranial morphological changes noticed during the agricultural transition (Walimbe and Tavares 1996), namely, gradual reduction in robusticity, smaller dentition (discussed later), straight or orthognathous face, reduction in cranial length value and corresponding increase in the cranial height, can very well be documented in the Kodumanal series. These changes have been attributed to three factors: decreased mechanical stress, increased nutritional stress, and higher infections (Walimbe 1998).

As stated above, it is better to recall the nature of the site. The people of the period I were predominantly artisans involved in bead manufacture

Fig. 4.6 Meg. IV: Triangular 'hole' on the cranial fragment (outer view).

Fig. 4.7 Meg. IV: Triangular 'hole' on the cranial fragment (inner view); note the scratch near the 'hole'.

and iron smelting, whereas the people of period II were predominantly agriculturists.

Metric observations made on this skeletal series are given in Table 4.1. For ready reference, part of the metric data published in the earlier report has also been included in the table.

Besides the morphometric observations discussed above, a few bone modifications need to be recorded. Some of these 'anomalies' could be pathological in origin; yet since the aetiology cannot be confirmed, these variations are included in this section.

Preservation status of Meg. IV is very fragmentary. The preserved cranial fragments show severe post-mortem damage of the outer table. The right side parietal, which is almost complete, shows very interesting morphology. It has a triangular *'hole'*, covering the approximate area of 8.26 X 8.13 mm (Fig. 4.6 and 4.7). There are faint 'scratch marks' (?) on the outer table, while on the inner table of the bone there are three small depressions surrounding the hole. It is rather difficult to explain this morphology. However, this 'act' seems to be done after the person had died. There is no new bone formation or any type of remoulding associated with it. In the absence of any such reaction, the possibility of its being

Fig. 4.8 Meg. IX-B: Root activity on the inner table of cranium.

some sort of antemortem 'surgical treatment' can be ruled out. It could also be insect hole or a perforation caused by a growing root. Incidentally, no other cranial bone of this specimen is preserved in good condition. Though the bone is undoubtedly human, it is unusually sturdy and gives almost metallic sound. The bone is covered with a thin layer of red sticky soil, which is hard to remove.

Meg. IX-B also exhibits very interesting morphological features along the inner table of the cranial vault. Starting from the right asterion, two very prominent and strong ridges are evident which run across the lambda point and further along the sagittal suture, resulting in a deep groove (Fig. 4.8). The feature is very prominently seen on the occiput than in the sagittal region. Though the groove is deep, its edges (in the form of ridges) are very sharp and defined and there is no new bone formation or any kind of bone change along the neighbouring bone tissue. The outer table along the affected area looks absolutely normal. There are no breaks seen along the bone either. This fact clearly indicates taphonomic origin of the 'lesion', most likely caused by vegetation growing in the area when the decomposing skeleton was not totally dried up.

Table No. 4.1 Craniometry of Kodumanal skeletal series

Measurement	Sp. I*	Sp. II*	Sp. III*	Meg. IX-A	Meg. IX-B	Meg. X-A	Trench ZJ 26, Sp. I	Trench ZJ 26, Sp. II	Trench ZJ 26, Sp. III
	Male 30-35 y	Female 25-20 y	(?) 5-6 y	Male 25-30 y	Female 18-20 y	Male 25-30 y	Child 7 y	Male 25 – 30 y	Child 13 – 14 y
Length Measurements on Neurocranium									
Maximum cranial length (1)	178	171	157	185	180	180	(165)	167	-
Glabella inion length (2)	157?	167	-	169	-	176	(138)	158	-
Glabella lambda length (3)	-	-	-	182	-	178	(145)	160	-
Breadth Measurements on Neurocranium									
Maximum cranial breadth (8)	135	116?	106	(135)	120	(125)	(120)	128	-
Minimum frontal breadth (9)	89	93	-	(97)	-	93	90	96	89
Maximum frontal breadth (10)	110	104	-	-	-	108	101	116	105
Bi-auricular breadth (11)	-	106	-	109	-	-	107	-	-
Greatest occipital breadth (12)	-	90?	-	113	-	-	103	108	-
Bi-mastoid breadth (13)	-	94?	-	99	-	-	93	-	-
Height Measurements on Neurocranium									
Basion-bregma height (17)	-	136	-	113	-	-	111	-	-
Auriculo bregmatic height (20)	100?	124	-	105	-	-	(113)	-	-
Calvarial height (22)				(85)	-	-	-	-	-
Circumference, Arc and Chord Measurements									
Horizontal circumference of skull (23)	510	486	-	(515)	-	(510)	-	(500)	-
Transverse arc (24b)	294	278?	-	(320)	-	-	(228)	-	-

Table 4.1 *contd.*

Measurement	**Sp. I***	**Sp. II***	**Sp. III***	**Meg. IX-A**	**Meg. IX-B**	**Meg. X-A**	**Trench ZJ 26, Sp. I**	**Trench ZJ 26, Sp. II**	**Trench ZJ 26, Sp. III**
	Male 30-35 y	**Female 25-20 y**	**(?) 5-6 y**	**Male 25-30 y**	**Female 18-20 y**	**Male 25-30 y**	**Child 7 y**	**Male 25 – 30 y**	**Child 13 – 14 y**
Longitudinal arc (25)	-	-		(365)	355	(380)	-	(325)	-
Frontal arc (26)	134	122	111	120	127	140	111	(115)	130
Parietal arc (27)	128	122	120?	(130)	117	140	(112)	125	-
Occipital arc (28)	110	108	-	(115)	111	(100)	(111)	(85)	-
Frontal chord (29)	114	107	94	105	(102)	112	(94)	(101)	110
Parietal chord (30)	112	108	106	(115)	105	121	103	106	-
Occipital chord (31)	97	87	-	(100)	95	(86)	87	(77)	-
Length Measurements on Face									
Facial length, facial depth (40)	-	104	-	(87)	-	-		-	-
Lower facial length (42)	-	-	-	92	-	-		-	-
Breadth Measurements on Face									
Outer bi-orbital breadth (43)	-	98?	-	113	-	-	91	-	95
Inner bi-orbital breadth (43-1)	95?	91?	-	105	-	-	84	-	87
Bi-orbital breadth (44)	-	-	-	101	-	-	(92)	-	83
Bi-zygomatic breadth (45)	-	-	-	124	-	-	(100)	-	105
Breadth of upper jaw (46)	-	86?	-	112	-	-	(72)	-	90
Height Measurements on Face									
Morphological facial height (47)	-	-	-	106	-	-	-	-	97
Upper facial height (48)	-	64	-	(59)	-	-	-	-	60

Table 4.1 *contd.*

Measurement	Sp. I*	Sp. II*	Sp. III*	Meg. IX-A	Meg. IX-B	Meg. X-A	Trench ZJ 26, Sp. I	Trench ZJ 26, Sp. II	Trench ZJ 26, Sp. III
	Male 30-35 y	**Female 25-20 y**	**(?) 5-6 y**	**Male 25-30 y**	**Female 18-20 y**	**Male 25-30 y**	**Child 7 y**	**Male 25-30 y**	**Child 13-14 y**
Measurements on Orbit and Inter-orbital region									
Anterior inter-orbital breadth (50)				27			-	-	21
Orbital breadth (51), right left	-	-37?	-	3838			-	-	3735
Orbital height (52), right left	-	3130	-	(34)(34)			(34)(34)	-	3232
Measurements on Nasal Region									
Nasal breadth (54)	-	27	-	28	-	-	-	-	23
Nasal height (55)	-	48	-	40	-	-	-	-	40
Measurements on Upper Jaw and Palate									
Length of upper jaw (60)	-	54	-	33	-	-	20	-	44
Breadth of upper jaw (61)	-	-	-	(57)	-	-	(52)	-	52
Sub-nasal height (48-1)	-	-	-	20	-	-	-	-	16
Palatal length (62)	42	36	-	(44)	-	-	-	-	(41)
Palatal breadth (63)	41?	35	-	38	-	-	-	-	32
External palatal arc (80)	-	-	-	(145)	-	-	100	-	120
Molar teeth row length (80-3), right	-	-	-	30	-	-	-	(26)	-
left	-	-	-	29	-	-	-	-	-
Premolar teeth row length [80-3a], right	-	-	-	13	-	-	-	-	-
left	-	-	-	12	-	-	-	-	-

Table 4.1 *contd.*

Measurement	Sp. I*	Sp. II*	Sp. III*	Meg. IX-A	Meg. IX-B	Meg. X-A	Trench ZJ 26, Sp. I	Trench ZJ 26, Sp. II	Trench ZJ 26, Sp. III
	Male 30-35 y	Female 25-20 y	(?) 5-6 y	Male 25-30 y	Female 18-20 y	Male 25-30 y	Child 7 y	Male 25-30 y	Child 13-14 y
Measurements on Lower Jaw									
Bi-condylar breadth (65)	-	96	23	-		-	-	-	88
Bi-coronoid breadth (65-1)	104	89	-	-		-	-	-	79
Bi-gonial breadth (66)	99	94	-	(90)	-	-	-	-	80
Bi-mental breadth, anterior	-	-	-	45	42	-	45	-	-
breadth (67)									
Length of lower jaw (68)	-	-	-	75	71	-	-	-	70
Condylo-symphyseal length (68-1), right	-	-	-	117	105	-	-	-	-
left	-	-	-	(117)	-	-	-	-	-
Chin height (69)	30	29	-	(27)	28	-	25	-	25
Condylar height (70), right	-	-	-	60	56	-	37	(52)	45
left	-	-	-	(60)	-	-	37	-	45
Height of coronoid (70-1), right	-	-	-	-	54	-	-	60	50
left	-	-	-	67	-	-	-	-	50
Ascending ramus minimum breadth (71), right	32	31	20	30	29	-	-	30	33
left	-	-	-	32	-	-	-	-	33

Table 4.1 *contd.*

Measurement	Sp. I*	Sp. II*	Sp. III*	Meg. IX-A	Meg. IX-B	Meg. X-A	Trench ZJ 26, Sp. I	Trench ZJ 26, Sp. II	Trench ZJ 26, Sp. III
	Male 30-35 y	Female 25-20 y	(?) 5-6 y	Male 25-30 y	Female 18-20 y	Male 25-30 y	Child 7 y	Male 25-30 y	Child 13-14 y
Ascending ramus maximum breadth (71-1), right	42	38	22	-	33	-	-	32	36
left	-	-	-	33	-	-	25	-	36
Condylo-coronoid breadth, right	-	-	-	-	31	-	-	30	34
left	-	-	-	(36)	-	-	26	-	34
External mandibular arc (80a)	-	-	-	200	-	-	-	-	170
Molar teeth row length [80-1a], right	-	-	-	32	-	-	-	33	-
left	-	-	-	32	-	-	-	-	-
Premolar teeth row length [80-b], right	-	-	-	13	15	-	-	-	-
left	-	-	-	14	-	-	-	-	-
Angles									
Total profile angle (72)	-	-	-	90	-	-	-	-	-
Nasal profile angle (73)	-	-	-	9.53	-	-	-	-	-
Alveolar profile angle (74)	-	-	-	84	-	-	-	-	-
Glabella-inion angle	-	-	-	8	-	-	-	-	-
Angles of superior facial triangle	-	-	-		-	-	-	-	-
n - ba - pr				32					
ba - pr - n				87					
pr - n - ba				61					

Table 4.1 *contd.*

Measurement	**Sp. I***	**Sp. II***	**Sp. III***	**Meg. IX-A**	**Meg. IX-B**	**Meg. X-A**	**Trench ZJ 26, Sp. I**	**Trench ZJ 26, Sp. II**	**Trench ZJ 26, Sp. III**
	Male 30-35 y	**Female 25-20 y**	**(?) 5-6 y**	**Male 25-30 y**	**Female 18-20 y**	**Male 25-30 y**	**Child 7 y**	**Male 25-30 y**	**Child 13-14 y**
Angles of cranial quadrilateral	-	-	-		-	-	-	-	-
l - ba - n				110					
ba - n - b				76					
n - b - l				112					
b - l - ba				62					
Mandibular angle (79), right	-	-	-	114	-	-	-	-	-
left	-	-	-	115	-	-	-	-	-
Indices									
Cranial capacity (Lee-Pearson 1901) (38)	-	1232.84	-	1275.30	-	-	-	-	-
Cranial index (I 1)	75.84	67.84?	67.52	72.97	-	69.44	72.72	76.64	-
Length-height cranial index, vertical index (I 2)	-	79.53	-	61.08	-	-	67.27	-	-
Breadth-height cranial index, trans. Vertical index (I 3)	-	117.24?	-	83.70	-	-	92.50	-	-
Auriculo-vertical index (I 4)	-	72.51	-	56.75	-	-	68.48	-	-
Calvarial height-breadth index (I 6)				62.96	-	-	-	-	-
Hauschild's circumference height index (I 9)	-	27.98	-	(21.94)	-	-	-	-	-
Sagittal arc index (I 10)	-	58.99?	-	(28.76)	-	-	-	-	-
Transverse frontal index (I 12)	80.91	89.42	-	-	-	-	89.10	82.75	84.76
Frontal index (I 13)	65.92	80.17?	-	71.85	-	-	75.00	76.12	-

Table 4.1 *contd.*

Measurement	Sp. I*	Sp. II*	Sp. III*	Meg. IX-A	Meg. IX-B	Meg. X-A	Trench ZJ 26, Sp. I	Trench ZJ 26, Sp. II	Trench ZJ 26, Sp. III
	Male 30-35 y	Female 25-20 y	(?) 5-6 y	Male 25-30 y	Female 18-20 y	Male 25-30 y	Child 7 y	Male 25-30 y	Child 13-14 y
Sagittal frontal index (I 22)	85.07	87.70	84.68	87.50	-	-	84.68	87.82	105.36
Sagittal parietal index (I 24)	87.50	88.52	88.33	88.46	-	-	91.96	80.08	-
Sagittal occipital index (I 25)	88.18	80.56	-	86.95	-	-	78.37	90.58	-
Foramen magnum index (I 33)	-	83.33	-	-	-	-	-	-	-
Skull modulus (I 37)	-	-	-	89.56	-	-	52.00	-	-
Total facial index (I 38)	-	-	-	85.48	-	-	-	-	92.38
Jugo-mandibular index (I 40)	-	-	-	72.58	-	-	-	-	76.19
Jugo-malar index (I 41)	-	-	-	80.64	-	-	-	-	85.71
Kollman's upper facial index (I 39)	-	-	-	47.58	-	-	-	-	57.14
Orbital index (I 42), right left	- -	- -	- -	89.47 89.47	- -	- -	- -	- -	86.48 91.42
Inter-orbital index (I 46a)	-	-	-	-	-	-	-	-	25.30
Nasal index (I 48)	-	56.62	-	57.14	-	-	-	-	57.50
Maxillo-alveolar index, Palato-alveolar index (I 54)	-	-	-	57.89	-	-	-	-	118.18
Transverse cranio-facial index (I 71)	-	-	-	91.85	-	-	-	-	-
Fronto-orbital index (I 72)	-	-	-	-	-	-	-	-	93.68
Jugo-frontal index (I 73)	-	-	-	78.22	-	-	-	-	84.76
Palatal height index (I 59)	-	-	-	-	-	-	-	-	28.12

* Measurements as calculated by Reddy-Reddy (1987)

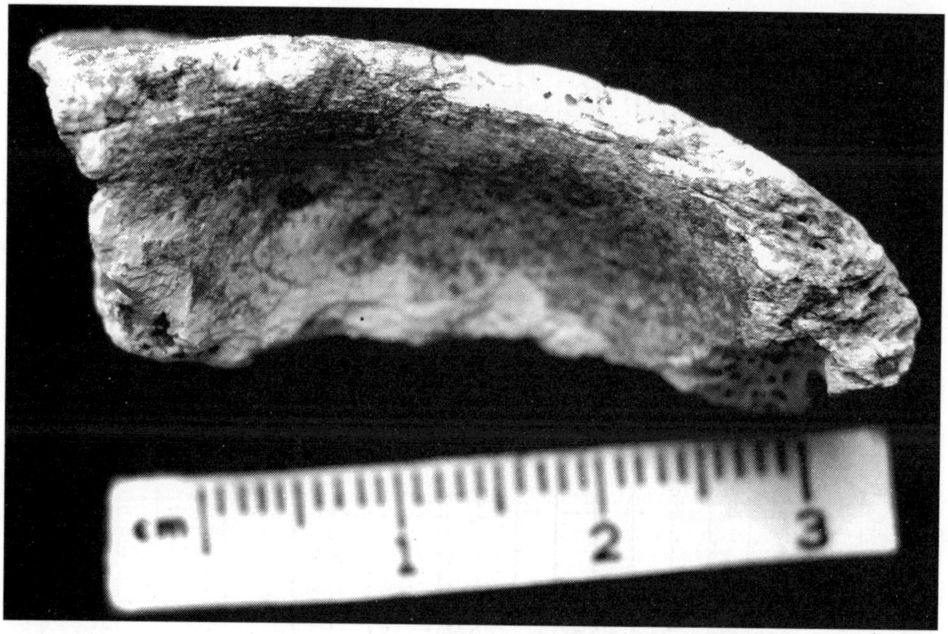

Fig. 4.9 Meg. X-B: Additional foramina on orbital roof.

For Meg. X, the preservation status is very fragmentary. Except the left orbital roof, no other bone from the facial skeleton is identifiable. Though many bones are represented in the skeleton, since the edges are weathered, reconstruction of the cranium is impossible. As mentioned earlier, the burial Meg. X consisted of two individuals, the cranium fragments were kept in one bag, and it appears that not all bone fragments were collected from the site. Consequently, there is a great deal of confusion in associating the bones as well as teeth individually. The association of dental and skeletal elements, as reported here, is based on gross morphological appearance of the fragments.

Of the two individuals from this burial, Meg. X-B, on its left orbital roof, inferiorly to the superior orbital foramen, exhibits two additional small-sized foramens (Fig. 4.9). No secondary bone formation is evident in and around these foramina and there is no indication of any post-mortem damage. These foramina are certainly morphological in origin, for passage of nerve and blood vessels. The right side bone is not available for comparison.

II. Post-cranial Elements

Post-cranial elements of the earlier series have not been subjected to close anthropological scrutiny in the earlier report (Reddy and Reddy 1987). Owing to the incompleteness of most of the bones, no meaningful osteometric data could be generated for these skeletal series. Fairly good estimate of maximum length is possible for some bones, which allows the estimating stature of the concerned individuals. Table 4 give details of stature estimation.

Table 4.2 Stature estimation

Sp. No	Bone	Side	Maximum length (cm)	Stature estimation (cm)	Mean (cm)
Meg. I, Sp. I (Male)	Humerus	R	(34)	175.17 ± 4.05	172.39
	Radius	R	(25)	173.51 ± 4.32	
	Femur	L	(45)	168.51 ± 3.27	
Meg. I, Sp. II (Female)	Humerus	L	(29)	155.41 ± 4.45	159.86
	Radius	R	(23)	163.95 ± 4.24	
	Tibia	L	(33)	160.23 ± 3.66	
Meg. IX-A (Male)	Humerus	R	(32)	169.01 ± 4.05	172.65
	Ulna	R	(27)	173.95 ± 4.32	
	Femur	R	(47)	173.27 ± 3.27	
	Tibia	R	(38)	174.38 ± 3.37	
Meg. IX-B (Female)	Radius	L	21	154.47± 4.24	155.22
	Ulna	L	23	155.97± 4.30	
Trench ZJ26 Sp. II: (Male)	Humerus	L	31.00	165.93 ± 4.05	177.47
	Radius	R	26.00	177.29 ± 4.32	
		L	26.50	179.18 ± 4.32	
	Ulna	R	28.00	177.65 ± 4.32	
		L	28.50	179.50 ± 4.32	
	Femur	L	(47.00)	173.27 ± 3.27	
	Tibia	R	(41.00)	181.94 ± 3.37	
		L	41.00	181.94 ± 3.37	
	Fibula	R	(40.00)	178.98 ± 3.29	
		L	(40.00)	178.98 ± 3.29	

In general, for the linear cranial measurements the male specimens give greater values than those for the female specimens. Yet, precise assessment of morphological bisexual disparity is not possible for cranial bones, since for most of the specimens anatomically distinguishing regions, like temporal line, orbital ridges, mastoid processes or nuchal area are either missing, broken or weathered. Noteworthy, nonetheless, is the mandible of the male individual, Meg. I, Sp. I; the bone is well built in the gonial and gnathion region. The ascending rami are also exceptionally broad with prominent condylar region.

Striking degree of sexual dimorphism is evident in the post-cranial elements of the Kodumanal series. All the crests, processes (esp. linea aspera), articular facets, etc. are prominent in male specimens in comparison to their appearance in females. Estimated stature for males is in the range of 172.39 cm (Meg. I, Sp. I) to 177.87 cm (ZJ26, Sp. II), while the two females, where calculations are possible, the height is 155.22 cm (Meg. IX-B) and 159.86 cm (Meg. I, Sp. II).

Following are a few additional morphological observations on the post-cranial elements.

Meg. IX-A

Right clavicle exhibits an anomalous feature. When compared with normal clavicular bones of the series and reference skeletons from the anthropology lab, this bone appears flattened along its anterior-inferior aspect near the sternal extremity. The inferior aspect of the bone from the lateral extremity, medially to conoid tubercle, has a robust looking bone formation. The affected area is approx. 1 cm and is evident as a groove-like feature. Aberrant morphological features on the bone could just be a normal morphological variation, but more likely an occupation-related change. Confirmation is not possible, as the left side bone is not preserved for comparison.

Right side ulna is complete, while the left side bone is damaged above the radial notch. The right bone is slightly thicker (R 2.1 cm, L 2.0 cm) than the left side showing bilateral asymmetry, which is in the normal range of variation.

The distal cap of R tibia is damaged but some portion is preserved and gives the evidence of squatting facet (Fig. 4.10). The distal extremity of the L side bone is not preserved in the collection. Occurrence of squatting

Fig. 4.10 Meg. IX-A: Squatting facet on R tibia.

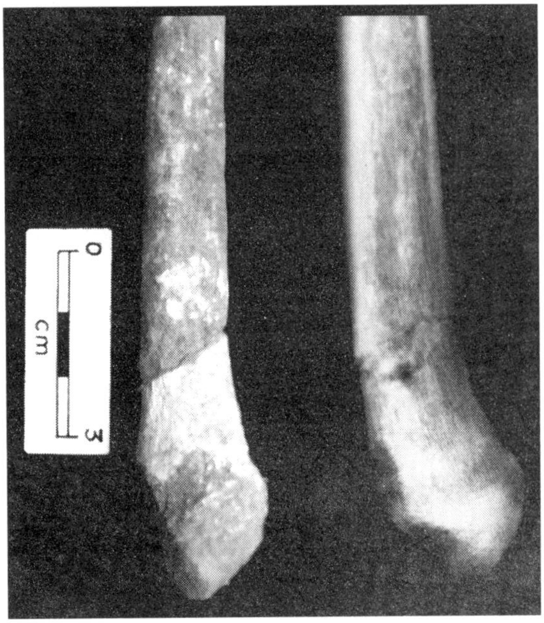

Fig. 4.11 IX-A: R fibula (bone and radiograph), note changed angle at distal end.

facets on the distal end of tibia is noteworthy among the protohistoric populations in the Indian sub-continent. In earlier populations and in modern primitive groups, where there is a lack of (or scarcity of) household furniture, the habit of squatting is normal; since the distal end of tibia comes in close contact with talus, the result may be the extension of certain articular surfaces or the development of new facets.

Interestingly, the R fibula shows changed angle of the bone along its distal extremity (Fig. 4.11). The bone is bent giving a concave appearance in the anterior perspective. Distal tibial articular surface appears slightly roundish, and interestingly along the medial aspect new bone formation is apparent in the form of longitudinal lines in the area of 3 cm, above the articular surface. The fibular articular surface of R tibia is damaged, preventing observation on the tibial involvement, if any. All the listed bone changes on the distal aspect of the fibula appear to be related to each other. It could be occupationally related resulting from a heavy mechanical strain. Also, possibility of a hair-line fracture cannot be ruled out; X-ray image of the bone hints the possibility. In either way, the damage probably resulted in defective tibia-fibula articulation.

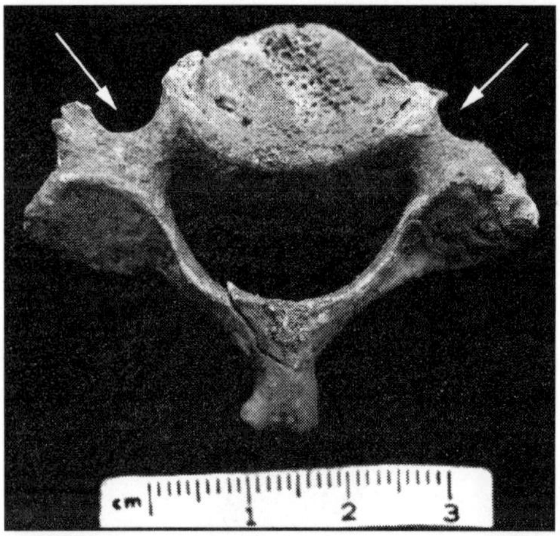

Fig. 4.12 Meg. IX-B: 5th cervical vertebra, note bilateral asymmetry in foramina.

Meg. IX-B

Preservation of this individual is fragmentary in nature. Only two long bones – L ulna (23 cm) and radius (21 cm) – are partially preserved to help estimate the height of the specimen. The estimations of stature on the basis of these two bones are 155.97$\pm$4.30 cm and 154.47$\pm$4.24 cm, respectively. The mean stature value of 155.22 cm is less, in comparison to the adult male specimens of the same series.

There are some incidences of morphological bilateral asymmetry in two of the vertebrae preserved for this individual. The two almost complete (but damaged in the pedicle region) vertebrae, tentatively identified as 5th and 7th from cervical region, exhibit different manifestations of morphological features bilaterally. The transverse foramina of the 5th vertebra shows differences in size (Fig. 4.12). Although the bone from left transverse process is broken, the outline of foramina seems to be bigger than that of the right side. For the 7th vertebra, a small ridge is evident on the inferior edge of the right superior articular surface, which is not prominently seen on the left side. At the same time, the angle in between pedicle and body from R side is deep and narrow in comparison to left side. Since there is no other kind of bone change in the region, these differential morphological expressions appear to be natural, and not because of any pathology.

Left side clavicle evidences slight bone thickening in the region of conoid tubercle. The thickness of the bone in the region for the R is 0.7 and for the L, it is 0.9 cm. Bilateral asymmetry is also seen in ulnar bones. The ridge, near the laterally placed radial notch from R side, is slightly elevated than the L side (Fig. 4.13).

No conclusive explanation can be given for the discrepancy seen in the element of the vertebral column. However, the clavicular change could be occupationally related. Several examples of morphological modifications in clavicle are known from the Indian protohistoric levels (Walimbe, *in press*). More discussion on this aspect appears in the pathology section.

Meg. X-A

There is no complete long bone to conduct metric analysis. Costalis tuberosity seen on the sternal end of left clavicular fragment is more prominent in comparison with that on the right side bone. Like other specimens, this could just be an example of bilateral asymmetry of morphological origin or it may have developed as a bodily response to occupational stress. The role of occupational stress cannot be confirmed due to the fragmentary condition of bones.

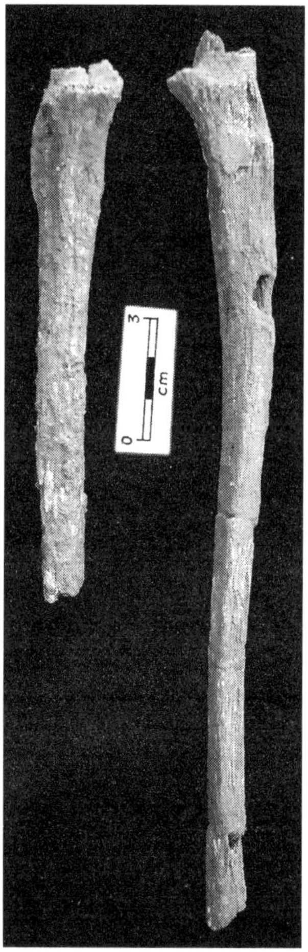

Fig. 4.13 Meg. IX-B: RL Ulna, note bilateral asymmetry near radial notch.

Meg. X-B

Very unusual lesion is seen on one of the bones of this individual. There is a probable evidence of intentional human activity on the broken shaft of distal left humerus, which measures 6.3 cm in length. The fragment includes the distal extremity where the portion from the beginning of olecranon fossa is missing. Approximately 4 cm of shaft is present. Along the superior edge of the broken shaft is an interesting evidence of 'cut mark'. The lesion is comparable with the 'pencil sharpened' bones reported from Kalpi (Walimbe 1999). The lesion is neatly made and polished, and is post-mortem in origin. The loss of olecranon region is also post-mortem in origin, but it cannot be related to the 'pathology' described above. No other portion of this bone is present in the collection. It may be mentioned that the right side humerus or other long bones preserved for this individual do not show this kind of 'lesion' (Figs. 4.14 and 4.15).

The lesion poses serious problems of interpretation. Several questions need to be answered while interpreting the marks.

Does any natural weathering process cause the marks? Or, are they rodent marks? If they indicate any intentional human activity, how these marks were made, and, more interestingly, why?

It is certain that the marks have appeared after the death of the individual. The bone was worked on after defleshing, but before they were

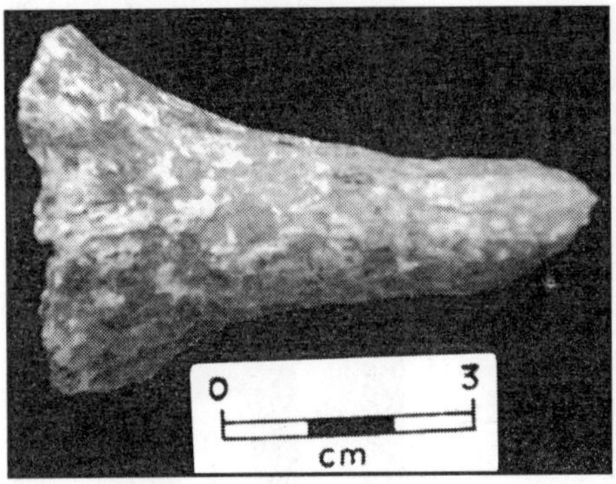

Fig. 4.14 Meg. X-B: L humerus.

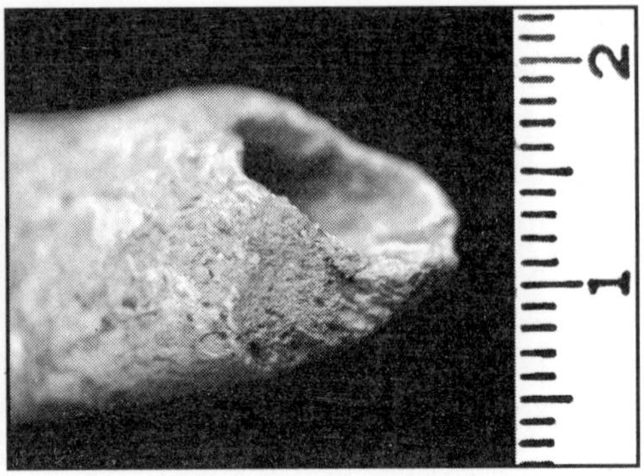

Fig. 4.15 Meg. X-B: L humerus, close-up of 'cut marks'.

completely dried up. In other words, the incident did not occur during the lifetime of the individual, or immediately after his death. This inference is based on three observations.

i. The activity area on the distal end looks very neatly and evenly worked. Such precision is difficult to achieve, even with a sharp metal weapon, when the bone is still embedded with muscles.
ii. Damage occurred to the distal extremity of the bone is in all probability a recent event. The elbow joint is quite deep and the bones, humerus and ulna are firmly held together in the trochlear region by strong muscle tendons. Removing the bone from this joint would require quite a long surgical procedure which is very hard to imagine in the population under investigation.
iii. The human activity appears to have been done before the bone was still not very old and totally dried. Working on dry bones would essentially result in 'chipping' at least on some occasions. The sharpening of the bone, on the other hand, looks quite smooth which is suggestive of the soft condition of the bone when they were being worked on.

The defleshing apparently had not been done with any stone tool as such activity would leave some marks and chipping on the bone. Nor other methods for defleshing, such as exposing or keeping the body in water currents, have been used. Under such event, one would expect signs of carnivore, vulture or fish activity. There are no charring marks on bone.

The fact that these skeletal remains have been recovered in the 'secondary' context, there could be another possibility. As per the field observations, the bones were not found in anatomical orientation but rather in a heap. It is possible, therefore, that the body was buried somewhere else in the first instance, the bones were removed at a later date, and ceremonially buried in this megalith.

Moreover, whether the bone was used as a tool is a question, which cannot be answered positively. It could be one unsuccessful attempt of tool making. Though the edge of the fragment is neatly 'sharpened', the working is not uniform on all sides, leaving one edge of the cut projecting. Such unevenly sharpened edges would not really justify use of the bone as a tool.

While concluding, yet another possibility needs to be stated. Around the edges of this cut, there are four minute slanting 'cut marks'. These marks are more or less parallel to each other, with a distance of less than 1 mm between them. While these marks can be taken as confirmation of human activity, at the same time, they might be taken as rodent gnawing marks. In that case, however, complete absence of proximal portion of the bone or totally normal appearance of other bones in that heap is difficult to explain.

The second author offers some explanation. All the burials exposed in the megalithic complex are secondary in nature. In the sense, the dead body is exposed earlier to nature and after some time, the left out bones have been collected and buried inside the cist. As the vulture marks are not found in the present study, it seems that the body had been exposed to nature but not to the vulture. It is very difficult to say categorically the method of defleshing at this moment. However, one may recall the description found in the Sangam literature dated early Christian era.

Tolkappiyam, the earliest Tamil grammar, speaks of the death rites performed during the erection of the burial as:

> *katchi kal kol nirpadai nadukal*
> *sir-t-taku sirappin perumpadai valttal*
>
> (*Tolkappiyam, Porul*.2-5)

In the context of the archaeological data, what we have at present is the information gathered from systematic exploration and scientific excavation of the material objects and the culture revealed by the megalithic monuments. It is hard to find material evidence to corroborate the literary data. *Katchi* probably meant 'lying in state' for some time, as is even now the practice, so that all the relatives and friends can assemble and do the ceremonial honour and wailing. *Kalkol*, likewise, probably meant the exposure of the body to the elements, as would be the case in excarnation; such post-excarnation or partial burial is clearly indicated by the many megalithic monuments excavated and studied. *Kal*, according to the contemporary *Paripadal* (3.88), meant 'the five elements'; the compound *kalkol* in that case meaning 'allowing the elements to take possession' and do their work or, in other words, to become one with the elements – *iyarkai eydutal*. *Nirpa-dai* would then refer to the ceremonial washing or purification of the few picked bones left after exposure at a much later date for its ceremonial burial, and *nadukal*, the erection of the stone (menhir) over it. This was to be followed by *perumpadai*, the great offering, perhaps with heaps of cooked rice (*perum-coru* in other contexts) and other food, and by *valttutal* – praise or adoration – perhaps with song (and dance).

Though we are not able to trace the names for each one of these several types from the earlier strata of the Sangam corpus, we have a few informative lines in a later epic *Manimekalai* (ch. 6.111.11.66-67) regarding the different modes of the disposal of the dead as:

suduvor iduvor todu kuli-p-paduppor
tal vayin adaippor taliyir kavippor

The context is the description of the great necropolis of the port city of Puhar or Kaverippattinam that adjoined the *Cakkaravalakkottam*, outside the city on the seashore. The lines quoted enumerate the different sets of people who came there for disposing off the dead with due rites and ceremonies, namely, those who cremated (*suduvor*), those who cast the cadaver or laid it for exposure to the elements for excarnation (*iduvor*), those who laid the body or mortal remains in pits dug into the ground for the purpose (*todu-kuli paduppar*), those who interred in subterranean cellars or cists (*tal vayin adaipoor*) and those who placed the body or the remains thereof inside a burial urn and inverted a lid over it (*taliyil-kavippor*). The first two modes hardly need any explanation. The third perhaps refers to total inhumation (if not partial), the fourth to cellars or tombs (*vayin*) let into the ground (*tal*), i.e., the stone cists and the like, in which the body or the remains of the exposure or cremation are interred, and the last mode, which though brief yet descriptive, refers to the placing of the corpse (total inhumation) or remains, thereof, into burial urns or sarcophagi (*tali*), the mouth of which was covered by the inverted lid (*kavi*).

Again, in an elegy on the Pandya king Nambi Nedum Celiyan, the poet Pereyin Muruvalar refers to different kinds of funerals, though not so clearly as in the *Manimekalai*.

iduka onro suduka onro
padu valip paduka venro

(*Purananuru* 239:20-21)

In the above lines, *iduka* would refer to exposure and burial, *suduka* to cremation or incineration and *paduvalip-paduka* to inhumation.

The above description clearly hints that the body was exposed for a certain amount of time as a part of a ritual. Whether the body is closed with leaves or covered with earth is hard to say. But one thing is clear that the body had not been exposed to the vultures as we did not find any reference in the literature as well as in the present study.

Trench ZJ26, Sp. II

Many of the long bones of this specimen are in better state of preservation and allow measuring maximum length. Though the stature estimates are already given in Table 4.2, relevant portion for this individual is reproduced here (Table 4.3) to explain the very unusual feature seen in this case. There is overall consistency in the stature estimates provided by radial and ulnar lengths, in the range of 177.25 to 179.50 cm. All the four bones are complete and there is no confusion regarding their length measurement. Left humerus of this individual is, however, relatively short. This complete and undamaged bone suggests stature of this individual as 165.93 cm, approximately 11 cm shorter than the estimates based on the bones of the lower segment. It may be noted that the right humerus is broken proximally from the region of 'anatomical neck', but matches in overall size with the left side bone, which confirms shorter upper arm on both the sides.

Similar anomaly is also noticed for the lower extremities. All the four bones of the lower segment are preserved. Though one or the other extremity is broken for these bones, fairly accurate estimate can be made for the maximum length. The stature figures, given by this segment, fall consistently in the range of 178.98 to 181.94 cm. Femur, however, is relatively shorter and gives a stature estimate of 173.27 cm. No explanation can be offered for this anomaly. It could be genetic deformity. There are no pathological markers seen on the bone.

This individual was buried in unusual *padmasana* posture. Is it in any way biological deformity used by this individual for achieving a different social status? Possibly not.

An ethno-archaeological study carried out by the second author during the course of excavation to understand the unusual posture (*padmasana* posture) offers some other explanation. It is learned that even today, the artisan family of the region bury their dead in the same way. It is interesting to note that the site of Kodumanal is known for artisans. The tradition would have been continued in this region till date. Therefore, the individual buried here probably comes from an artisan family.

Nevertheless, the mean stature of this individual, 177.87 cm, is comparable with other male individuals from this series.

Also, morphological changes are seen on the right and left clavicle of this individual. The right bone shows moderately developed plate near the sternal end, which is expressed as a rugged area or muscle marking. It also exhibits moderate robusticity near the conoid tubercle and prominent ridge on the inferior aspect of the bone. There are depressions on both clavicles near the sternal end.

Table 4.3 Stature estimation for Specimen ZJ26, Sp. II

Bone	Side	Length in cm	Stature estimation cm
Humerus	L	31.00	165.93 ± 4.05
Radius	R L	26.00 26.50	177.29 ± 4.32 179.18 ± 4.32
Ulna	R L	28.00 28.50	177.65 ± 4.32 179.50 ± 4.32
Femur	L	(47.00)	173.27 ± 3.27
Tibia	R L	(41.00) (41.00)	181.94 ± 3.37 181.94 ± 3.37
Fibula	R L	(40.00) (40.00)	178.98 ± 3.29 178.98 ± 3.29
Mean stature		177.47 cm	

B. Description of Dental Elements

Dental inventory includes 191 teeth as specified in Table 6. In brief, the sample comprises 103 maxillary and 88 mandibular, and 22 deciduous and 169 permanent teeth. Details of dental inventory are given in Table 4.4.

The observations conducted include metric and morphological assessment of occlusal features.

Table 4.4 Dental elements included in the study

Specimen no	Deciduous				Permanent				Total
	Maxillary		Mandibular		Maxillary		Mandibular		
	R	L	R	L	R	L	R	L	
Meg. I, Sp. I	-	-	-	-	4	6	8	8	26
Meg. I, Sp. II	-	-	-	-	5	1	-	-	6
Meg. I, Sp. III-A	1	-		-	-	-	-	-	1
Meg. I, Sp. III-B	-	-	1	-	-	-	-	-	1
Meg. IV	-	-	-	-	6	3	5	2	16
Meg. V	-	-	-	-	1	1	-	-	2
Meg. IX A	-	-	-	-	6	4	5	3	18
Meg. IX-B*	-	-	-	-	6	6	5	2	19
Meg. X-A	-	-	-	-	5	3	7	4	19
Meg. X-B **	-	-	-	-	3	1	4	1	9
Trench ZJ26, Sp. I	5	3	5	4	4	2	2	2	27
Trench ZJ26, Sp. II	-	-	-	-	8	8	6	2	24
Trench ZJ26, Sp. III	-	1	1	1	4	6	4	6	23
Sub-Total	6	4	7	5	52	41	46	30	191
Total	10		12		93		76		191
Grand total	22				169				191

* Identification of RM3 is uncertain.

** Exact association and identification of two molars, tentatively identified as maxillary RM3 and mandibular RM2, presumed to be of this individual, is not certain.

I. Metric Analysis

All measurable teeth are included in the analysis. Out of 191 teeth present in this series, 131 are measurable. Dental remains of two individuals, Trench ZJ26, Sp. I and Trench ZJ26, Sp. III are not measured.

Table 4.5a and 4.5b give the basis odontometric data.

For maxillary teeth, mesial members of each tooth class (I1, Pm1 and M1) are generally larger in crown dimensions than the distal members of the same tooth class. For this general trend, however, some exceptions are noted. For example, the maxillary third molars of male specimen

Table 4.5a Odontometric data for maxillary dentition

Tooth		Meg. IV (M)		Meg. IX-A (M)		Meg. IX-B (F)		Meg. X-A (M)		Meg. X-B (F)		Meg. I, Sp. I (M)		Meg. I, Sp. II (F)		Trench ZJ26, Sp. II, (M)	
		R	L	R	L	R	L	R	L	R	L	R	L	R	L	R	L
I1	MD	-	8.39	-	-	8.36	8.36	-	-	-	-	-	-	-	-	-	9.16
	BL	-	7.11	-	-	7.40	7.40	-	-	-	-	-	-	-	-	-	6.95
	CA	-	59.55	-	-	61.86	62.01	-	-	-	-	-	-	-	-	-	63.66
	CI	-	118.00	-	-	112.97	113.24	-	-	-	-	-	-	-	-	-	131.798
	CM	-	7.75	-	-	7.88	7.89	-	-	-	-	-	-	-	-	-	.05
I2	MD	-	6.62	-	-	6.84	6.58	7.14	-	-	-	-	7.08	-	-	-	7.20
	BL	-	6.04	-	-	6.73	6.88	7.44	-	-	-	-	7.24	-	-	-	7.52
	CA	-	39.98	-	-	46.03	45.27	53.12	-	-	-	-	51.25	-	-	-	54.14
	CI	-	109.60	-	-	101.63	95.63	95.96	-	-	-	-	97.79	-	-	-	95.74
	CM	-	6.33	-	-	6.78	6.73	7.29	-	-	-	-	7.16	-	-	-	7.36
C	MD	7.33	7.39	-	-	-	-	-	-	-	-	8.12	8.09	-	-	7.65	7.30
	BL	8.05	8.04	-	-	-	-	-	-	-	-	8.70	8.72	-	-	8.22	8.18
	CA	59.00	59.41	-	-	-	-	-	-	-	-	70.64	70.54	-	-	62.88	59.71
	CI	91.05	91.91	-	-	-	-	-	-	-	-	93.33	92.77	-	-	93.06	89.24
	CM	7.69	7.71	-	-	-	-	-	-	-	-	8.41	8.40	-	-	7.93	7.74
Pm1	MD	6.97	-	6.72	6.71	6.60	6.66	6.32	-	-	-	7.04	7.04	6.81	-	-	6.70
	BL	8.86	-	8.35	8.35	8.92	8.95	8.66	-	-	-	10.23	10.25	8.75	-	-	9.46
	CA	61.75	-	56.11	56.02	58.87	59.60	54.73	-	-	-	72.01	72.16	59.58	-	-	63.38
	CI	78.66	-	80.47	80.35	73.74	74.41	72.97	-	-	-	68.81	68.68	77.82	-	-	70.82
	CM	7.91	-	7.53	7.53	7.76	7.81	7.49	-	-	-	8.63	8.64	7.78	-	-	8.08

Table 4.5a *contd.*

Pm2	MD	6.94	-	6.22	-	6.19	-	6.39	6.39	6.97	-	-	6.38	6.08	6.06	6.64	6.63
	BL	8.88	-	8.69	-	8.96	-	8.66	8.65	8.72	-	-	9.81	8.70	8.73	9.35	9.48
	CA	61.62	-	54.05	-	55.46	-	55.33	55.27	60.77	-	-	62.58	52.89	52.90	62.08	62.85
	CI	78.15	-	71.57	-	69.08	-	73.78	73.87	79.93	-	-	65.03	69.88	69.41	71.01	69.93
	CM	7.91	-	7.45	-	7.57	-	7.52	7.52	7.84	-	-	8.09	7.39	7.39	7.99	8.05
M1	MD	9.86	-	10.59	10.31	10.29	10.30	10.20	10.18	-	-	10.33	10.34	9.29	-	10.71	10.86
	BL	11.03	-	10.79	10.73	10.80	10.85	10.19	10.16	-	-	10.14	10.13	10.47	-	11.42	11.21
	CA	108.75	-	114.26	110.62	111.13	111.75	103.93	103.42	-	-	104.74	104.74	97.26	-	122.30	121.74
	CI	89.39	-	98.14	96.08	95.27	94.93	100.09	100.19	-	-	101.87	102.07	88.72	-	93.78	96.87
	CM	10.44	-	10.69	10.52	10.54	10.57	10.19	10.17	-	-	10.23	10.23	9.88	-	11.06	11.03
M2	MD	7.98	-	8.56	8.58	8.56	8.91	-	9.39	-	9.28	10.11	10.22	9.36	-	8.23	8.64
	BL	11.01	-	10.92	10.78	10.44	10.59	-	9.74	-	10.24	10.24	10.27	(10.49)	-	10.28	10.29
	CA	87.85	-	93.47	92.49	89.36	84.13	-	91.45	-	95.02	103.52	104.95	98.18	-	84.60	88.90
	CI	72.47	-	78.38	79.59	81.99	84.13	-	96.40	-	90.62	98.73	99.51	89.22	-	80.05	83.96
	CM	9.49	-	9.74	9.68	9.50	9.75	-	9.56	-	9.76	10.17	10.24	9.92	-	9.25	9.46
M3	MD	7.35	-	8.18	8.20	-	-	9.50	-	9.03	-	-	-	8.88	-	7.91	7.91
	BL	10.46	-	11.66	11.76	-	-	9.11	-	11.28	-	-	-	10.32	-	10.23	10.15
	CA	76.88	-	95.37	96.43	-	-	86.54	-	101.85	-	-	-	91.64	-	80.91	80.28
	CI	70.88	-	70.15	69.72	-	-	104.28	-	80.05	-	-	-	86.04	-	77.32	77.93
	CM	8.90	-	9.92	9.98	-	-	9.30	-	10.15	-	-	-	9.60	-	9.07	9.03

Table 4.5b Odontometric data for mandibular dentition

Tooth		Meg. IV (M)		Meg. IX-A (M)		Meg. IX-B (F)		Meg. X-A (M)		Meg. X-B (F)		Meg. I, Sp. I (M)		Meg. I, Sp. II (F)		Trench ZJ26, Sp. II, (M)	
		R	L	R	L	R	L	R	L	R	L	R	L	R	L	R	L
I1	MD	-	-	-	-	-	-	5.12	5.70	-	-	4.88	4.95	-	-	6.17	5.83
	BL	-	-	-	-	-	-	5.37	5.56	-	-	5.77	5.79	-	-	6.36	6.09
	CA	-	-	-	-	-	-	27.49	31.69	-	-	28.15	28.66	-	-	39.24	35.50
	CI	-	-	-	-	-	-	95.34	102.51	-	-	84.57	85.49	-	-	97.01	95.73
	CM	-	-	-	-	-	-	5.24	5.63	-	-	5.32	5.37	-	-	6.26	5.96
I2	MD	-	-	-	-	5.95	-	6.34	6.44	-	-	5.87	5.74	-	-	6.84	-
	BL	-	-	-	-	5.52	-	6.60	6.80	-	-	5.77	5.80	-	-	6.29	-
	CA	-	-	-	-	32.84	-	41.84	43.79	-	-	33.86	33.29	-	-	43.02	-
	CI	-	-	-	-	107.78	-	96.06	94.70	-	-	101.73	98.96	-	-	108.74	-
	CM	-	-	-	-	5.73	-	6.47	6.62	-	-	5.82	5.77	-	-	6.56	-
C	MD	6.30	-	-	-	6.23	-	7.46	-	-	-	6.86	6.58	-	-	7.42	-
	BL	6.82	-	-	-	7.02	-	7.14	-	-	-	6.25	6.29	-	-	-	-
	CA	42.96	-	-	-	43.73	-	53.26	-	-	-	42.87	41.38	-	-	-	-
	CI	92.37	-	-	-	88.74	-	104.48	-	-	-	109.76	104.61	-	-	-	-
	CM	6.56	-	-	-	6.62	-	7.30	-	-	-	6.55	6.43	-	-	-	-
Pm1	MD	7.00	-	6.89	-	6.10	-	6.36	-	6.94	-	6.57	6.59	-	-	-	7.13
	BL	7.20	-	7.29	-	7.33	-	7.27	-	7.16	-	7.66	7.80	-	-	-	7.92
	CA	50.40	-	50.22	-	44.71	-	46.23	-	46.69	-	50.32	51.40	-	-	-	56.46
	CI	97.22	-	94.51	-	83.21	-	87.48	-	96.92	-	85.77	84.48	-	-	-	90.02
	CM	7.10	-	7.09	-	6.71	-	6.81	-	7.05	-	7.11	7.19	-	-	-	7.52

Table 4.5b *contd.*

Pm2	MD	7.14	-	6.70	-	6.45	-	6.80	-	7.04	-	6.46	6.60	-	-	-	-
	BL	7.53	-	7.50	-	7.37	-	7.92	-	7.45	-	7.81	7.82	-	-	-	-
	CA	53.76	-	50.25	-	47.53	-	53.85	-	52.44	-	50.45	51.61	-	-	-	-
	CI	94.82	-	89.33	-	87.51	-	85.85	-	94.49	-	82.71	84.39	-	-	-	-
	CM	7.33	-	7.10	-	6.91	-	7.36	-	7.24	-	7.13	7.21	-	-	-	-
M1	MD	-	11.63	10.75	10.77	10.38	10.34	10.58	10.58	11.00	10.84	10.90	10.75	-	-	11.84	-
	BL	-	10.49	10.23	10.29	9.77	9.84	10.26	10.25	9.25	9.25	9.90	9.96	-	-	10.38	-
	CA	-	121.99	109.97	110.82	101.41	101.74	108.55	108.44	101.75	100.27	107.91	107.07	-	-	122.89	-
	CI	-	110.86	105.08	104.66	106.24	105.08	103.11	103.21	118.91	117.18	110.10	107.93	-	-	114.06	-
	CM	-	11.06	10.49	10.53	10.07	10.09	10.42	10.42	10.12	10.04	10.40	10.35	-	-	11.11	-
M2	MD	10.96	11.10	9.75	9.73	9.66	-	10.23	10.01	10.32	-	9.78	9.90	-	-	10.21	-
	BL	9.72	9.57	9.18	9.17	9.05	-	9.08	8.99	9.53	-	9.82	9.76	-	-	10.18	-
	CA	104.88	100.22	89.50	89.22	87.42	-	92.88	89.98	98.34	-	96.03	96.62	-	-	103.93	-
	CI	112.75	115.98	106.20	106.10	106.74	-	112.66	111.34	108.28	-	99.59	101.43	-	-	100.29	-
	CM	10.34	10.33	9.46	9.45	9.35	-	9.65	9.50	9.92	-	9.80	9.83	-	-	10.19	-
M3	MD	9.64	-	9.28	9.29	-	-	-	-	-	-	9.71	9.95	-	-	11.10	-
	BL	9.82	-	9.16	9.17	-	-	-	-	-	-	9.87	9.86	-	-	10.35	-
	CA	94.66	-	85.00	85.18	-	-	-	-	-	-	95.83	98.10	-	-	114.88	-
	CI	98.16	-	101.31	101.30	-	-	-	-	-	-	98.37	100.91	-	-	107.24	-
	CM	9.73	-	9.22	9.23	-	-	-	-	-	-	9.79	9.90	-	-	10.72	-

Meg. IX-A have larger breadth dimension than that of M2s. Similar trend is noted for the female specimen Meg. X-B, where the RM3 is exhibits greater BL value than the LM2. Meg. I, Sp. I also has broader RLM2s than LM1, though the difference is marginal. The greater breadth values for the teeth noted above are reflected in giving greater crown area values for the respective comparison.

In mandibular dentition, third molars of two specimens (Meg. I, Sp. I and Trench ZJ26, Sp. II) are larger than their second molars. Second premolars in most of the cases are larger than the first premolars. A similar trend is also seen for incisors where I2s are larger than I1s.

Both maxillary and mandibular first molars of specimen Trench ZJ26, Sp. II are largest in the series. Though mandibular second and third molars of this specimen are larger than the other individuals, interestingly maxillary second and third molars are the smallest (except two cases, RM3 of Meg. IV and LM2 of Meg. IX-B).

It is also interesting to note that there is a trend as seen usually in males having greater crown dimensions than females. Two notable observations, which go against this statement, are the larger M1s of IX-B, where crown area is in the range of 111.13 to 111.75, as against the crown areas for two male specimens (Meg. I, Sp. I and Meg. X-A) where the crown areas are 103.93-103.42 and 104.74, respectively. No clear pattern for sexual dimorphism emerges when crown indices are compared.

Twenty-two deciduous teeth are present in the collection. They are not subjected to metric analysis.

Comparison of dental features among different archaeological populations and interpreting the patterns in relation to the life-ways of these extinct populations provides interesting information. As indicated above, the crown area, the product of mesio-distal and bucco-lingual diameter, is the best indicator for tooth size assessment.

The total molar crown area calculation is possible for three individuals of this series. This data is compared with the MCA values reported for various archaeological populations representing different cultural levels, viz., the Mesolithic, Harappan, Neolithic, Chalcolithic, Iron Age Megalithic, and Historic. MCA values for some recent populations have also been used.[1] Because of the statistical inadequacy of the sample, there are several limitations in drawing precise comparative picture. Nevertheless, broader knowledge can be gained using these tables. Table 4.6 gives the total molar crown area (MCA) values for selected archaeological populations.

The mean MCA value for the three male individuals from Kodumanal is 604.03 mm^2 (range 587.57 to 629.51 mm^2). Among the populations compared, the highest MCA value is obtained for the Mesolithic Langhnaj and the lowest for the Historic Kuntasi.

Table 4.6 Molar crown area (MCA) for selected sites in decreasing order

Culture	Site	MCA
Mesolithic	Langhnaj	756.01
Chalcolithic	Daimabad	726.23
Mesolithic	Bellan Bandi Palassa	702 46
Neolithic	Mehrgarh	697.74
Mesolithic	Bagor	695.10
Megalithic	Mahurjhari	675.54
Chalcolithic	Inamgaon	671.38
Modern	Gond (M)	661.23
Chalcolithic Megalithic	Banahali	654.74
Chalcolithic	Nevasa	642.91
Megalithic	Timargarh	642.45
Megalithic	Pomparippu	625.00
Modern	Mahadev Koli (M)	623.89
Megalithic	Sarai Khola	613.52
Harappan	Harappa	606.32
Historic	Jotsoma	606.25
Megalithic	Kodumanal	604.03
Historic	Padri	602.80
Modern	Gond (F)	597.07
Modern	Mahar (M)	597.24
Megalithic	Hullikallu	592.79
Modern	Maratha (M)	575.54
Modern	Mahadev Koli (F)	572.96.
Harappan	Rupar	563.98
Mesolithic	Sarai Nahar Rai	563.76
Modern	Mahar (F)	561.20
Neolithic	Burzahom	559.99
Modern	Maratha (F)	546.60
Historic	Kuntasi	517.49

Note: Table is modified after Lukacs (1985b) and Walimbe-Kulkarni (1993).

The Mesolithic, Neolithic and Chalcolithic populations have MCA values of more than 640, except for that of Sarai Nahar Rai and Burzahom (563.76 and 559.99, respectively). The Harappan populations have molar size smaller than that of the Megalithic sites (MCA values 606.32 for Harappa and 563.98 for Rupar). The Daimabad specimen represents the Late Harappan phase of the Chalcolithic culture. This phase has not yielded much evidence of agriculture (Sali 1986). The subsistence was probably on both hunting and gathering with agricultural supplementation. The larger crown area of Daimabad specimen could be attributed to such mixed economy. No explanation can, however, be given for the smaller molar size area of the Mesolithic Sarai Nahar Rai or Neolithic Burzahom. Sarai Nahar Rai skeletons are characterized by large and muscular robust cranial and post-cranial features and tall stature (Kennedy *et al.* 1986). The discrepancy in dental size and body size is difficult to explain. At Burzahom also, hunting and gathering way of life could be established on the basis of cultural antiquity. There is no evidence of agriculture or even for the domestication of animals. The smallest (in the series) dental size of Burzahom specimen does not fit in this context. The Harappan culture is essentially an urban culture. The smaller dental size in Harappans could be interpreted as an urban adaptation of the population for the soft and processed food. High incidence of caries among Harappans supports the hypothesis of food economy consisting of more carbohydrate food than meat.

The MCA of Kodumanal series, 604.03 mm^2, is based on 3 male specimens. Smaller teeth of Kodumanal than many of the megalithic sites could be because of their greater dependence on agriculture and use of sophisticated implements for food preparation. The site of Kodumanal is rich in cultural artefacts, reflecting the elegant lifestyle of their possessors. The less masticatory stress might have acted as a selective force for influencing biology.

No individual of the Kodumanal series preserves full dentition. Consequently, the total crown area (TCA), sum of the cross-sectional area of the crowns of upper and lower teeth on one side of the dental arcade, cannot be calculated.

Inferences drawn from these comparisons, however, are not to be stretched too far. For most of the populations, sample being small in size, data for male and female individuals is pooled. In such cases, the mean values are obviously to some extent influenced by smaller dental size in females. It may be noted that sexual dimorphism in dental size expression is well documented by Walimbe and Kulkarni (1993). Moreover, '*representativeness*' of the sample becomes doubtful due to smaller sample size. Furthermore, the sites are widely separated occupying diverse geographical areas and have evidenced racial differences in the skeletal morphology, etc. Lastly, different scholars have studied dental sample, and therefore personal error is bound to be reflected in recording. The problems of sampling error and personal error are to some extent nullified if the data is 'pooled' culture-wise. Therefore, to summarize the discussion, the 'pooled' MCA values are given in Table 4.7.

Table 4.7 Culture-wise pooled MCA values

Culture	MCA
Mesolithic	673
Neolithic	668
Bronze Age	645
Chalcolithic	699
Megalithic	639
Modern	597

Miscellaneous Indices

Calculations have been done for Incisor Breadth Index (IBI), Molarisation Index (MI), and Step Index (SI). Though comparisons have not been attempted with other archaeological or living populations, the data is reported here for future reference.

Incisor Breadth Index (IBI)

It may be noted that generally maxillary lateral incisor is broad in Asian populations than the European populations. As a result for most of the Asian populations, IBI value is reported in the range of 0.82 to 0.87, while for Europeans the focal value is reported to be 0.76 (Lukacs 1985a). The Kodumanal specimens have mean IBI of 80.49 (Table 4.8).

Molarisation Index (MI)

The molarisation index is generally high in maxillary dentition than for the mandible. For the Kodumanal series (Table 4.9), the general range of maxillary MI is 0.81 to 0.97, whereas for mandible, the value fluctuates between 0.73 to 0.81. The higher values of MI indicate greater degree of molarisation of second premolar.

Table 4.8 Incisor Breadth Index

Sp. No	Maxilla	
	R	L
Meg. IV	-	93.10
Meg. IX-B	81.81	78.52
Trench ZJ26, Sp. I	75.12	-
Trench ZJ26, Sp. II	-	78.60
Trench ZJ26, Sp. III	-	75.84

Table 4.9 Molarisation Index

Sp. No	Maxilla		Mandible	
	R	L	R	L
Meg. I, Sp. I	-	96.84	78.80	78.51
Meg. I, Sp. II	83.09	-	-	-
Meg. IV	80.50	-	-	-
Meg. IX-A	80.53	-	73.31	-
Meg. IX-B	82.96	-	75.43	-
Meg. X-A	84.98	85.13	77.19	-
Meg. X-B	-	-	80.54	-
Trench ZJ26, Sp. II	81.87	84.87	-	-

Table 4.10 Step Index: M3

Sp. No	Maxilla		Mandible	
	R	L	R	L
Meg. I, Sp. I	-	-	99.69	98.69
Meg. I, Sp. II	98.56	-	-	-
Meg. IV	94.83	-	-	-
Meg. IX-A	108.98	109.09	89.54	89.11
Meg. X-A	89.40	-	-	-
Trench ZJ26, Sp. II	89.57	90.54	99.71	

Step Index (SI)

In the living populations, where results are based on sufficient sample size, more consistency is seen for the step index. In archaeological populations in certain cases, like Bellan Bandi Palassa, Langhnaj, Hullikallu or Pomparippu, the bucco-lingual diameter of third molar or second molars are more or almost equal to that of the first molar. In general, greater reduction tendencies in bucco-lingual diameter are seen in mandibular dentition than maxillary. Though not used for comparative study, just for record the values of step index for M2 and M3 are given in tables 4.10 and 4.11.

Table 4.11 Step Index: M2

Sp. No	Maxilla		Mandible	
	R	L	R	L
Meg. I, Sp. I	100.98	101.38	99.19	97.99
Meg. I, Sp. II	100.19	-	-	-
Meg. IV	99.81	-	-	91.22
Meg. IX-A	101.20	100.46	89.73	89.11
Meg. IX-B	96.66	97.60	92.63	-
Meg. X-A	-	95.86	88.49	87.70
Meg. X-B	-	-	103.02	-
Trench ZJ26, Sp. I	104.22	102.11	93.54	-
Trench ZJ26, Sp. II	99.51	91.79	98.07	-
Trench ZJ26, Sp. III	83.64	-	-	94.77

II. Morphology

Morphological assessment has been done only for the molar teeth. In total, 69 teeth are assessed for the morphological pattern on their occlusal surface. The incidence of commonly observed morphological features has been noted. The traits observed are: Maxillary molars: hypocone, metacone, metaconule and Carabelli's trait. Mandibular molars: cusp number, groove pattern and expression of the 5th cusp for the lower molars. The observations are given in Table 4.12.

In general, hypocone, metacone and Metaconule expression is more pronounced in the first and second molars. The Carabelli cusp, an additional cusp seen on the lingual side of mesiolingual cusp of upper molars, is developed only in Meg. IX-A male specimen (see Fig. 4.3). The expression is of Grade 5 on the right first molar, where a small cusp without a free apex occurs. Carabelli on the left molar is of Grade 3, where the trait occurs as a small Y-shaped depression. It may be noted that the frequency of Carabelli cusp can be used for population comparison, provided the sample size is large.

Other than common morphological features, parastyle is noted on maxillary RM2 of specimen IX-A, which is an uncommon trait. Parastyle

Table 4.12 Dental Morphology

Trait	Side	Meg. I, Sp. I			Meg. I, Sp. II			Meg. IV			Meg. IX-A			Meg. IX-B		
Maxilla		M1	M2	M3	M1	M2	M3	M1	M2	M3	M1	M2	M3	M1	M2	M3
Hypocone	R	5	3	-	?	?	?	4	0	2?	5	0	3?	4	?	?
	L	5	3	-	-	-	-	-	-	-	5	0	4?	4	?	-
Metacone	R	4	4	-	4	4	2	5	4	3	5	4	5	5	4	?
	L	4	4	-	-	-	-	-	-	-	5	4	5	5	5	-
Metaconule	R	0	0	-	0	0	0	0	0	0	3	1	?	0	1	?
	L	0	0	-	-	-	-	-	-	-	3	?	?	0	4	-
Carabelli's cusp	R	0	0	-	0	0	0	0	0	0	0	0	0	0	0	0
	L	0	0	-	-	-	-	-	-	-	0	0	0	0	0	-
Mandible																
Groove pattern	R	Y	+	+	-	-	-	-	+	X	+	+	+	+	+	-
	L	+	+	+	-	-	-	?	+	-	+	+	+	+	-	-
Cusp number	R	5	4	4	-	-	-	-	4	4	4	4	4	4	4	-
	L	4	4	4	-	-	-	?	4	-	4	4	4	4	-	-
Cusp 5	R	3	0	0	-	-	-	-	0	0	0	0	0	0	0	-
	L	0	0	0	-	-	-	0	0	-	0	0	0	0	-	-

Table 4.12 Dental Morphology *contd.*

Trait	Side	Meg. X-A			Meg. X-B			Tr. ZJ 26, Sp. I			Tr. ZJ 26, Sp.II			Tr. ZJ 26, Sp.III		
Maxilla		M1	M2	M3	M1	M2	M3	M1	M2	M3	M1	M2	M3	M1	M2	M3
Hypocone	R	5	-		-	-	-	3.5	5	-	4	3	1	4	3.5	-
	L	5	5		-	4	-	4	5	-	4	3	1	4	-	-
Metacone	R	5	-		-	-	-	4	4	-	5	4	3	3.5	3.5	-
	L	5	5		-	2?	-	4	4	-	5	4	3	4	-	-
Metaconule	R	2	-		-	-	-	0	0	-	3	0	3	0	0	-
	L	3	0		-	0	-	0	0	-	3	0	3	0	-	-
Carabelli's cusp	R	5	-		-	-	-	0	0	-	0	0	0	0	0	-
	L	3	0		-	0	-	0	0	-	0	0	0	0	-	-
Mandible																
Groove pattern	R	Y	+	-	Y	-	-	+	-	-	Y	+	+	+	-	-
	L	Y	+	-	Y	-	-	+	+	-	-	-	-	+	+	-
Cusp number	R	5	4	-	5	-	-	4	-	-	5	4	4	4	-	-
	L	5	4	-	5	-	-	4	4	-	-	-	-	4	4	-
Cusp 5	R	3	0	-	3	-	-	0	-	-	4	0	0	0	-	-
	L	3	0	-	0	-	-	0	0	-	-	-	-	0	0	-

is mostly seen on the buccal surface of the mesiobuccal cusp (the paracone or cusp 2) of the third molar. However, it can also occur on the other molars in the same location, but is less frequent. In this specimen, the feature appears as a small cusp with an attached apex and can be graded as '2'.

Another worth notable morphology is the bilateral asymmetry seen on the maxillary RLI2 of Meg. IX-B. The MD (mesio-distal) distance of R and L is 6.84 and 6.58 mm, respectively, resulting in the short length of the crown for the left side. Opposite to this, the BL (bucco-lingual) distance of crown for R and L is 6.73 and 6.88 mm, respectively.

For mandible, all the molars (M1, M2, and M3) from both side exhibit '+' type groove pattern and the cusp number is also '4'. There is no extra cusp in any of the molars. There is a fossa 1.0 mm above the cemento-enamel junction (CEJ) on mandibular RM2 of Meg. X-A on the buccal side of the crown, where C1 and C3 cusps meet each other. For LM2, the feature is seen only as a line in the same area.

Another notable feature which needs to be noted is remoulding of dental crown on the mesial aspect of maxillary LI2 of specimen Meg. IX-B. There is a groove on the edge of the mesial aspect measuring 0.90 mm, approx. 2.52 mm above the CEJ. There is also no evidence of infection or caries. The neighbouring tooth LI1 does not show any indication of enamel remoulding of its distal aspect. The lesion on the lateral incisor could be due to deliberate human act, possibly because of habitual cleaning of tooth by using tread. Such prolonged activity may result into formation of such deep groove on the crown, which looks like a hook when the tooth is viewed in its anatomical position. It may be noted that in contemporary peasant societies, cleaning tooth/teeth with tread is commonly seen.

C. Pathology

Besides the morphological discrepancies of bilateral size variation in clavicle, which could be occupation related (e.g. Sp. IX-A, IX-B, and X-A), 'cut-marks' on humerus of X-B, and possible hair-line fracture in fibula of IX A, there are a few examples of pathologies seen on this skeletal series. These anomalies and lesions are described in this section.

As mentioned earlier, bones and teeth are covered with preservative coating precluding minute observations on the bone changes. Nevertheless a few convincing pathological markers are discernable in the collection.

Prominent pathological lesions / anomalies observed on this series include markers of specific/non-specific infections, like maxillary sinusitis, periostitis, porotic hyperostosis, degenerative pathologies like vertebral lipping, dental pathologies like enamel hypoplasia, tartar accumulation,

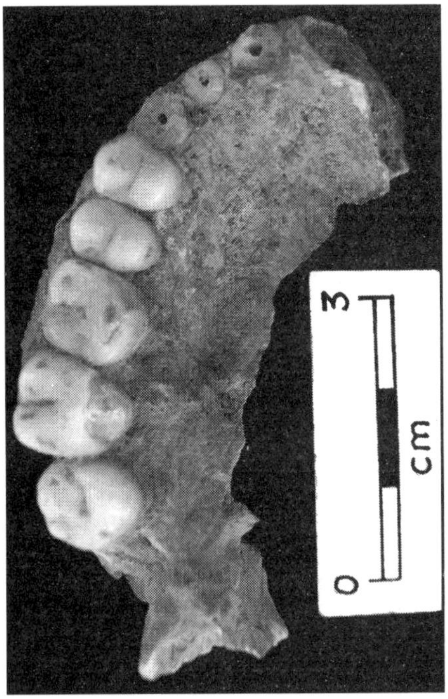

Fig. 4.16 Meg. I, Sp. II: R Maxilla, occlusal view.

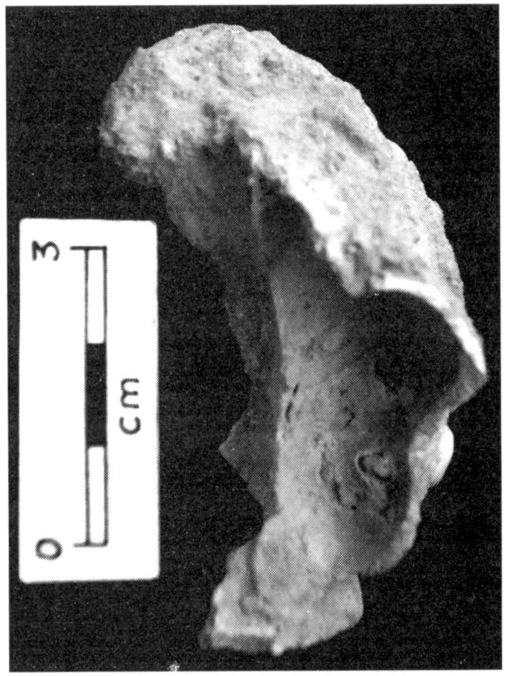

Fig. 4.17 Meg. I, Sp. II: R Maxilla, superior view, note infection on maxillary floor.

attrition, dental crowding and asymmetry. Few morphological changes, for which etiology of occupational stress cannot be ruled out, have been described earlier.

Maxillary Sinusitis

Of the nine adult specimens of the Kodumanal series, maxillary bone(s) are preserved for six individuals. Sinus floor, maxillary surface potential for sinusitis, is observable in all these specimens, of which the lesion of maxillary sinusitis is observed in three individuals, two confirmed and one doubtful case.

Meg. I, Sp. II

This individual is a female and was around 30 to 35 years old at the time of death. Right maxillary fragment with five teeth *in situ* is preserved in the collection (Fig. 4.16). The broken state of fragment allows direct inspection of the floor (Fig. 4.17). Slight resorption of floor with some bone remoulding appears on the maxillary sinus floor. This area has also

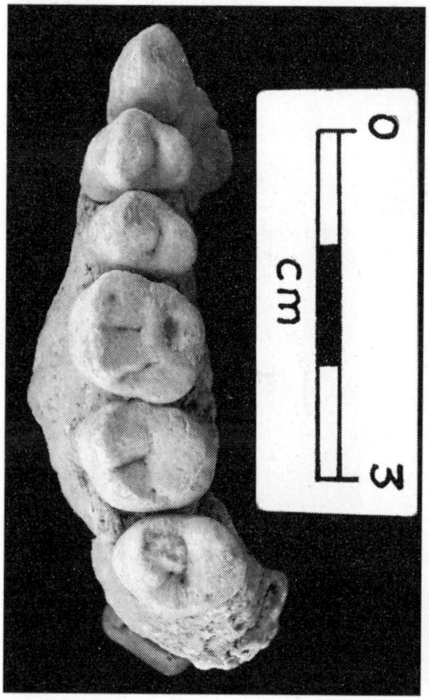

Fig. 4.18 Meg. IV: R Maxilla, occlusal view.

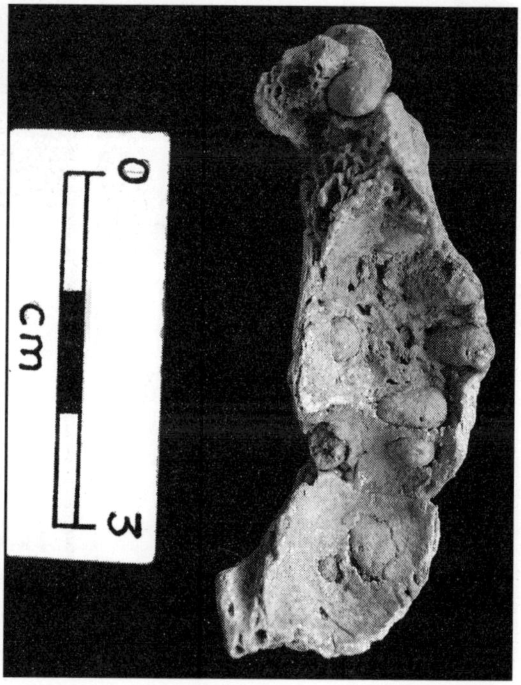

Fig. 4.19 Meg. IV: R Maxilla, superior view, note infection on maxillary floor.

suffered from post-mortem damage resulting in exposure of molar root tips on this floor. The changes are very minute and because of the post-mortem damage, no positive diagnosis is possible. It may be noted that the molar teeth of this individuals also slight to moderately worn out. No other pathology is seen in dentition.

Meg. IV

This individual is a male aged around 25 to 30 years. Broken fragment of right maxilla with six teeth *in situ* is preserved for this individual (Fig. 4.18). Direct inspection of the floor is possible in this specimen. The right side maxillary floor gives an evidence of bone remoulding in the area of around 1 cm above the RPm1 and M1, exposing roots of these teeth on the maxillary sinus floor (Fig. 4.19). The floor above M2 and M3 looks normal in texture. Left side bone is not preserved for comparison. None of the molars show significant attrition, which confirms no role of dentition in the bone change. The possible aetiology of this lesion can, therefore, be attributed to airborne infection.

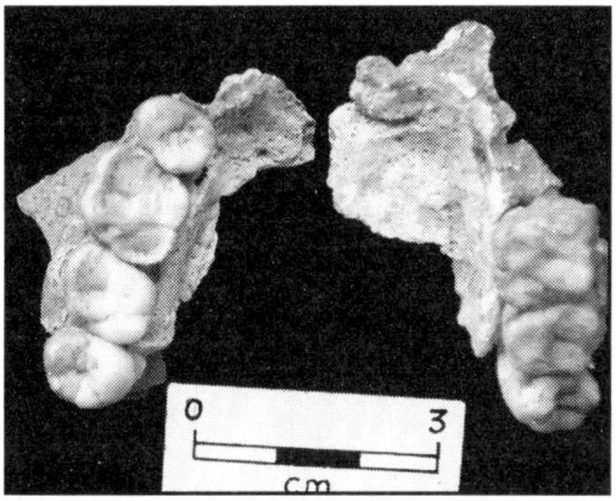

Fig. 4.20 Trench ZJ26, Sp. II: Maxilla, occlusal view.

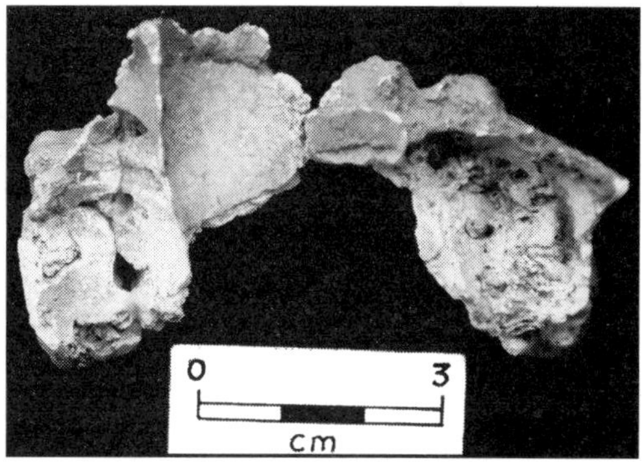

Fig. 4.21 Trench ZJ26, Sp. II: Maxilla, superior view, note infection on maxillary floor.

Trench ZJ 26, Sp. II

This is a male individual also died around the age of 30 years. Both maxillary sinus floors are preserved in the collection and can be inspected directly. Confirmed diagnosis of maxillary sinusitis can be made for the right side bone. The complete sinus floor from Pm2 to M3 shows severe amount to bone remoulding involving an area of around 3 cm. Roots of these teeth are exposed on the floor (Fig. 4.20 and 4.21). On the left side bone, slight porosity is seen above the Pm2. Dentition shows only moderate amount of attrition, which indicates that the lesion on the right maxillary sinus floor is more likely to have been caused by airborne infection.

Maxillary sinusitis is an infectious disease, which affects the area of maxillary sinus floor. It is broadly defined as inflammation of the mucosa of the paranasal sinuses. It functions as the body's first defence against airborne particulate and pathogens. When disruption of bone starts, it results in the inflammatory events. Chronic or repeated inflammation of the sinus mucosa may result in damage to the surrounding bony tissue (Merrett and Pfeiffer 2000). The maxillary sinuses are relatively inaccessible to direct examination, making them difficult to study.

Usually pathogens inhaled into the maxillary sinus may cause primary infection within the sinus. Another route for this infection is through the floor of the sinuses from periapical abscessing and periodontal disease. The thin layer of bone between the apex of the molar roots and the maxillary sinus may be resorbed as a result of periapical abscessing. Destruction of bone may also occur if excessive force is applied during tooth extraction (Merrett and Pfeiffer 2000). As stated earlier, the lesion seen in Kodumanal specimens cannot be attributed to dental problem.

Sinusitis caused by airborne factors may be a result of crowded dwellings, poor sanitation, presence of accompanying respiratory infection, chronic exposure to dense smoke and the quality of the fuel. It gives information about the respiratory health status of past human population.

Of the three cases of maxillary sinusitis noted in the Kodumanal series, the bone changes in the female individual appears doubtful, whereas the lesions observed on two male individuals are of confirmed nature. Both the cases are related to airborne infection due to chronic smoke inhalation.

The doubtful appearance of infection on female specimen (Meg. I, Sp. II) can be attributed to smoke inhalation for cooking in closed walls. Similar incidences have been noted in the early agro-pastoral communities of the Deccan Plateau, and in some medieval and historic populations as well (Reddy 2002). Ethnoarchaeological studies documenting air pollution level in the kitchen while cooking are supportive of this conclusion.

The pathology in male specimens is also airborne, but could be occupation related. The Iron Age Megalithic population of Kodumanal might have been in iron smelting and iron tool making profession. Though direct correlation cannot be established, smoke from the iron furnace could be taken as a probable cause. Though in no way a causative factor for sinusitis, the bone changes in the shoulder region seen in one of these individuals are worth recording. As stated earlier, the clavicles of specimen ZJ26, Sp. II display bilateral asymmetry (Fig. 4.22). The right bone shows moderately developed plate near the sternal end, which is expressed as a rugged area or muscle marking. It also exhibits moderate robusticity near the conoid tubercle and prominent ridge on the inferior aspect of the bone. There are depressions on both clavicles near the sternal end. These changes in the clavicle are occupation related, cased by repetitive movements of certain body parts. For example, in this case using right arm repeatedly for blowing air to furnace while shaping tools can be taken as a causative factor. Skeletal markers of occupational stress can clarify the daily activity patterns of individuals. These include a variety of activity-induced changes produced by stress on human bone. Continual stress of a muscle in repetitive tasks creates a well-preserved skeletal record of an individual's habitual activity patterns. Robusticity markers seen in the clavicle of specimen ZJ26, Sp. II can be taken as a normal reaction of the skeleton to habitual muscle usage, reflecting daily activities that produce rugged markings at the musculoskeletal site of attachment.

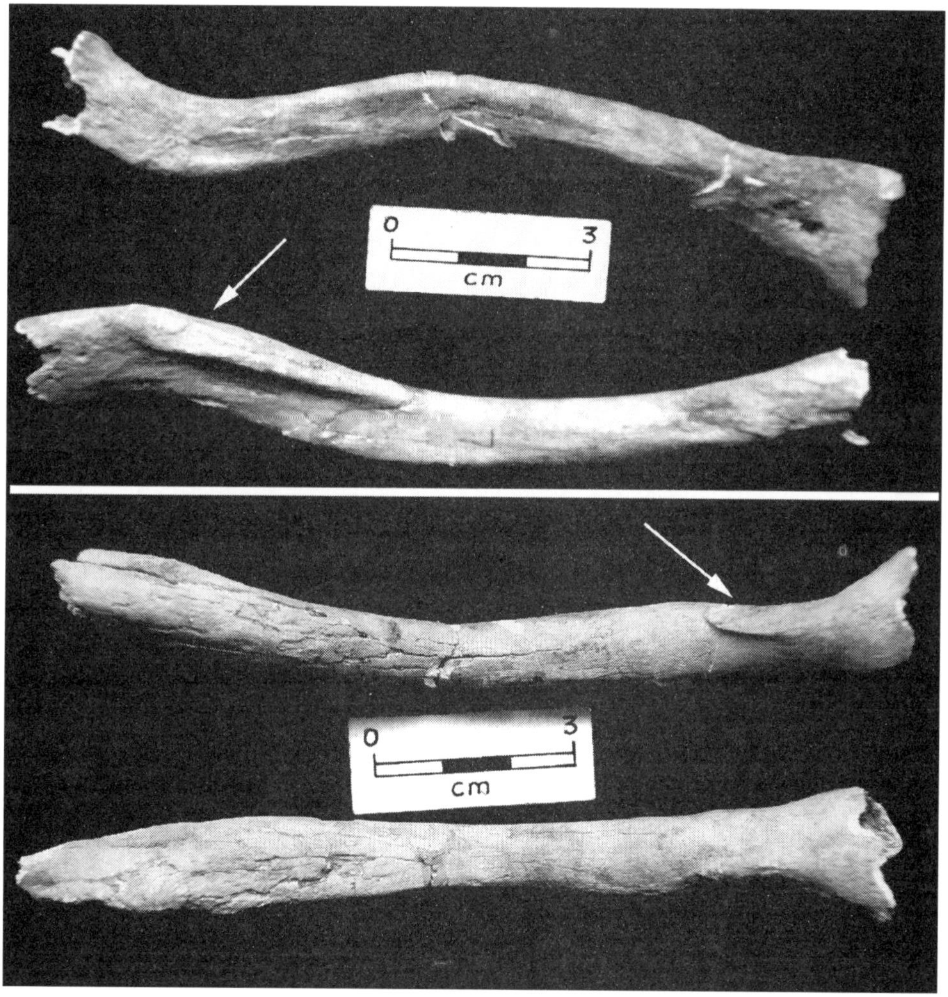

Fig. 4.22 Trench ZJ26, Sp. II: RL clavicles, note habitual stress markers.

Occurrence of clavicular change and deformed maxillary floor might not be just a co-incidence, but strongly point to occupation-related airborne infection.

Non-specific Infections

Two other types of pathological lesions are noted in the Kodumanal series which can be grouped under 'non-specific infection' category. These are periostosis and porotic hyperostosis.

Periostosis, as a disease by itself, is uncommon. It usually represents part of, or a reaction to, pathologic changes of the underlying bone. Bone, because of its continued ostoblastic capacity (new cell formation), reacts to many different insults with formation of woven bone. This new bone formation is not always an expression of inflammation but is just one of the reactions to any specific or nonspecific infections of bone. The new bone formation, if continues over a long period of time, makes the bone surface irregular and affects the bone thickness as well. The marked, uneven hypervascularity visible on dry bone in the form of smaller and larger pores in periosteal bone is often striking (Ortner and Putschar 1981).

Mid-shaft fragment of fibula preserved for Meg. I, Sp. III-B shows new bone formation which can be interpreted as periostitis. Incidentally, the bone is broken allowing seeing the bone section very clearly. Extent of the bone affected cannot be judged precisely as the bone is covered with preservative coating and matrix precluding inspecting the lesion from the outer table. Apparently, there is no indication of new bone formation on this surface.

The second type of non-specific pathology, primarily caused due to nutritional deficiency, is porotic hyperostosis.

Sufficient quantity of minerals is required for healthy growth of the body. Iron constitutes the main component of an average diet and is an important element in haemoglobin, which helps to transport oxygen to the blood tissue. It also contributes to the strength of the immune system. A good amount of iron is provided by animal as well as plant foods. However, phytates, plant proteins, or intestinal parasitic infections hinder iron absorption (Baynes and Brothwell 1990). In clinical terms, iron deficiency is not a disease by itself, but is only a symptom, which results in lack of colour, reduction of size and life span of red blood cell size. But iron-deficient individuals become prone to catch recurrent infection. In general, children have a greater risk of experiencing iron deficiency than adults. During infancy, body mass increases very rapidly and if the child is fed exclusively on breast milk the iron demand is not fulfilled.

Skeletal manifestations of this pathological lesion can be diagnosed in the prehistoric populations. However, causative factors for this pathology cannot be precisely deduced. The range, besides iron deficiency, includes sickle cell anaemia or thalassemia, and loads of intestinal parasites. The bone changes are related to a hyperactive bone marrow that creates pressure on surrounding bone, increasing the width of the marrow space and decreasing width of the outer table of bone. The most evident manifestation of the lesion appears as a normal smooth and dense outer compact bone (parietal or orbit are the most commonly affected bones of skull) is pitted by small holes of varying size and density. If the lesion appears on orbital roof, it is commonly referred to as *cribra orbitalia*. The lesion may have bilateral appearance, as seen in the Kodumanal specimen, or may have asymmetrical expression.

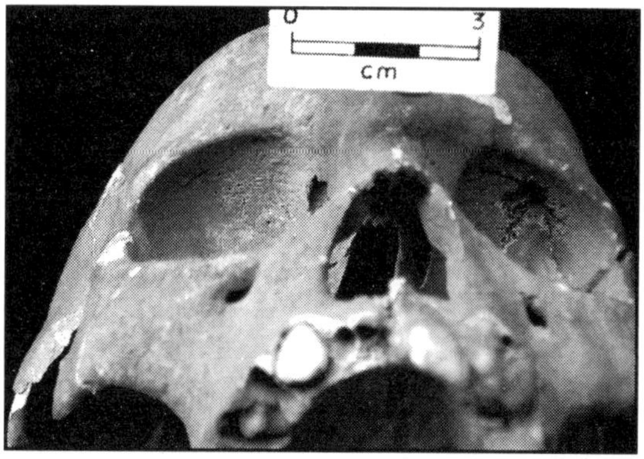

Fig. 4.23 Trench ZJ26, Sp. III: Cribra orbitalia on RL orbital roof.

Both right and left orbital roofs of ZJ26, Sp. III are preserved in the collection and both give evidence of porosity (Fig. 4.23). The traces of porosity can be identified on the roof, where approx. 1 x 1 cm area is affected on the right side. Area of porosity of the left side cannot be measured accurately as the bone suffers post-mortem damage. It may be noted that this individual also shows evidence of disturbed dental eruption sequence in both maxilla and mandible. Both these factors point out that this individual was probably suffering from some nutritional deficiency.

Vertebral Pathology

Meg. I, Sp. I

Complete vertebral column has suffered from medium to severe post-mortem damage precluding detailed pathological observation. Yet, moderate amount of osteophytic growth is seen on three vertebral bodies, two from the thoracic region (cannot be individually identified) and one from the lumber region (2nd lumber). It is quite difficult to comment on the involvement of any other vertebra.

Meg. 1, Sp. II

There is only one thoracic vertebra preserved in better state. The left side superior articular surface of this vertebra is morphologically different than the right side. This left side articular surface is split in between. No new bone formation is seen in the affected area. Since no other vertebra from the thoracic region is preserved in the collection, the reason behind this anomaly cannot be diagnosed.

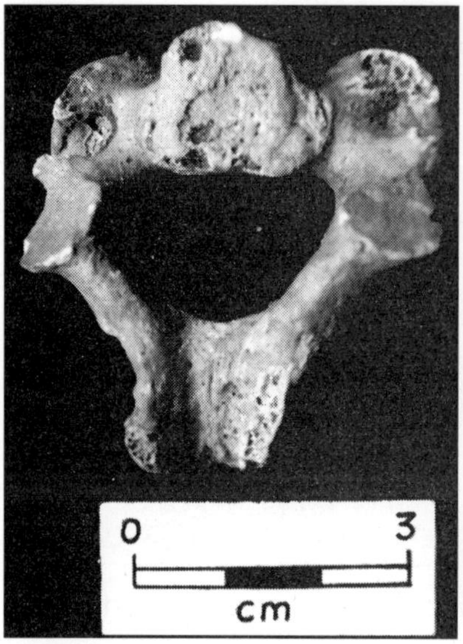

Fig. 4.24 Trench ZJ26, Sp. II: Axis (inferior view), note osteophytic growth on vertebral body.

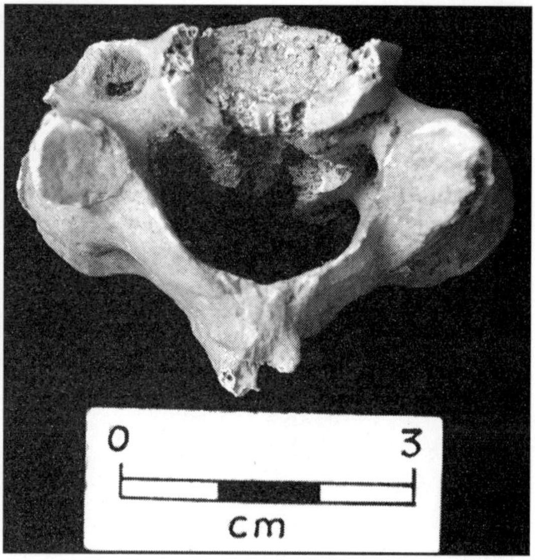

Fig. 4.25 Trench ZJ26, Sp. II: 3rd cervical (superior view), note osteophytic growth on vertebral body.

Trench ZJ26, Sp. II

The vertebral column of this individual shows joint-related pathological problems. The inferior aspect of body of second cervical (axis) and the superior side of third cervical vertebra indicates moderate new bone formation (Fig. 4.24). It is quite evident on the axis, but the feature is not easily distinguishable because of the post-mortem damage to the third cervical. The bone modification, if any, of inferior aspect of the third vertebra is not observable since the fourth cervical is stuck with the third one (Fig. 4.25). There is no bone formation on the superior aspect of axis and inferior aspect of atlas vertebra.

Another joint-related problem seen in three vertebral bodies, probably from the mid-thoracic region. Since only bodies of these vertebrae are preserved, no individual identification of the elements affected is possible; probably they represent the 5th, 6th, and 7th thoracic (Fig. 4.26). There is new bone formation on the superior and inferior aspects of the vertebral bodies. There is also occurrence of 'Schormal nodes' on the inferior surface of the 5th and superior surface of the 6th.

The feature of spinal osteophytosis seen on the vertebrae of the thoracic and lumber region can be taken as a degenerative pathology. Gradual deterioration with advancing age affects all elements of the skeletal system,

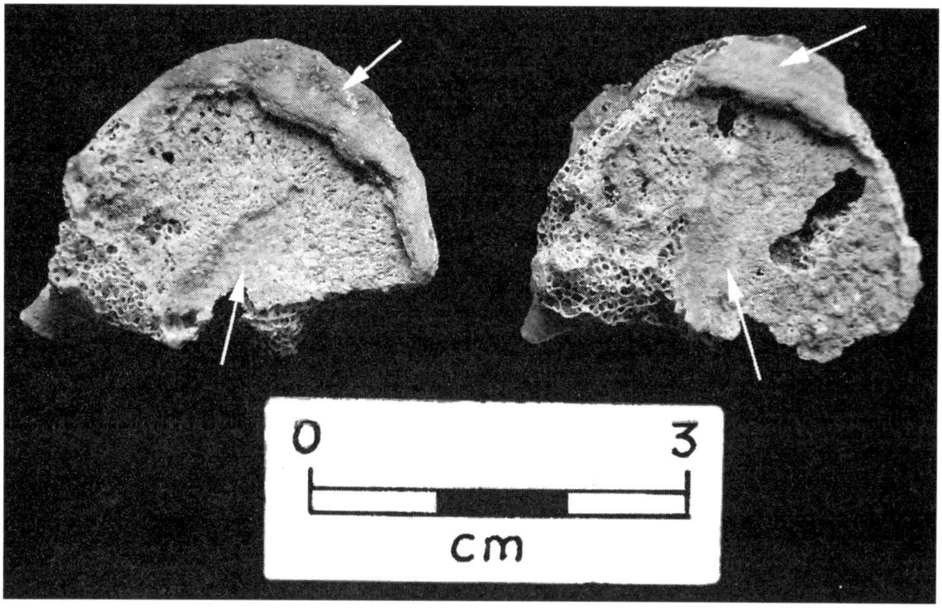

Fig. 4.26 Trench ZJ26, Sp. II: Thoracic vertebrae, note osteophytic growth and Schormal's node on vertebral body.

more particularly the joints and the vertebral column. The continuous mechanical stress and strain on each segment of the spine is one of the major penalties paid by humans for their adoption of the erect bipedal posture (Roberts and Manchester 1995). In the aging process, chemical and degenerative changes occur in the fibrous inter-vertebral discs, causing their rupture and resulting in growth of bone from the margins of the vertebral bodies. This growth of bone (osteophytosis), if continues further, results in union of adjoining vertebrae and gradual fixing of the spinal segment and preventing movement. The condition seen in the Kodumanal specimens might not be very serious but it must have been quite painful with backache, and probably stiffness, affecting inefficiency in performing activities that require bending of the axial skeleton.

Also interesting to note that Schormal's nodes, which occur as a result of intervertebral disc pressure on the vertebral bodies, are associated with other forms of degenerative change. Specific aetiology for these nodes is unknown but they are taken as the result of pressure exerted by disc contents on the vertebral body surfaces (Sanuja *et al.* 1986, *quoted in* Roberts and Manchester 1995). Trauma (stress fracture) has also been taken as one of the causes for this condition. Prolong pressure weakens the bone structure enabling Schmorl's nodes to develop.

Dental Anomalies

Dentition is constructed of dense and hard material and therefore resists decay in the ground. It constitutes one of the most important components of physical evidence for bygone human populations. Studies on dental remains are important in archaeological perspectives. The mouth functions primarily as a food processor and food type determines the micro-organisms present in the mouth. The condition of a person's teeth, therefore, reflects the composition of the food that has come into contact with those teeth. As Lukacs (1989) points out, dentition provides information on the composition of diet of early man (what is eaten), nutrition (physiological adequacy of the diet), and subsistence (method of procuring the diet) of prehistoric populations. Dental pathology is the scientific study of the origin, nature, and course of dental diseases and associated diseases of jaws. It illustrates the complexity of bio-cultural (or genetic-environmental) interaction in prehistoric human populations.

Kodumanal dental series comprises healthy teeth. No infectious diseases, like caries or periodontal lesions, are recorded. There are a few noteworthy pathologies and anomalies, which following Lukacs (1989), can be grouped as: 1. Degenerative diseases, displaying loss of a conspicuous amount of tooth or bone surface or substance, these are observed in the form of varying degrees of attrition of occlusal surface; 2. Developmental diseases, effecting or influencing formation of dental tissues or developing interrelationship between teeth and their supporting structures, the jaws; these kinds of pathologies appear in the Kodumanal series as bilateral discrepancy in eruption process, dental crowding, etc. In one specimen, tartar accumulation is observed.

The following is the description of individual pathologies.

Attrition

Dental attrition is the gradual and regular loss of tooth substance as a result of natural mastication (Pindborg 1970). It is a mechanical process, reflecting daily and intimate contact of the people with their environment. Attrition of the occlusal surfaces may destroy the enamel, exposing the underlying dentine. Attrition continued beyond this point may threaten exposure of the pulp cavity. Dental attrition is the most commonly reported phenomenon in archaeological skeletal studies. In addition to the attrition resulting from natural mastication, several other factors also contribute to attrition. For example, occlusal inaccuracy resulting from antemortem tooth loss, occupation-related stress, preference for a side for chewing and hygienic habits of the individual contribute in accelerating the attrition rate.

The quality and quantity of abrasives in the diet is also considered as a major influencing factor. Hard, fibrous and unprocessed food of the Mesolithic hunter-gathers or processed soft food of the early agricultural societies is stated to have different kind of occlusal wear pattern.

Slight to severe type of attrition is noted on the preserved sets of teeth, which have been graded following Buikstra and Ubelaker (1994). The data for attrition on the permanent molar teeth is given in Table 4.13.

Table 4.13 Grades of attrition on the permanent molar teeth

Sp. No.	Age	Sex	Maxilla						Mandible					
			M1		M2		M3		M1		M2		M3	
			R	L	R	L	R	L	R	L	R	L	R	L
Meg. IV	Adult	M	5	-	4	-	0	-	-	5	4	4	0	-
Meg. IX-A	Adult	M	4	4	2	3	1	1	4	4	2	2	1	1
Meg. IX-B	Adult	F	0	0	0	0	-	-	1	2	-	1	-	-
Meg. X-A	Adult	M	1	1	-	1	0	-	3	3	1	1	-	-
Meg. X-B	Adult	F	-	-	1	1	-	-	0	0	0	-	-	-

Meg. IV

Dentition shows slight to moderate degree of attrition. Maxillary LI1 and LI2 give 'grade 3' attrition. Though the maxillary right canine does not have any wear, the left canine shows 'grade 4'. Maxillary right first and second molars indicate 'grade 5 and 4', respectively (see Fig. 4.18). The third molar from the same side does not show any attrition. For mandible, attrition on LM1 and RLM2s is of 'grade 5' and grade '3', respectively.

Meg. X-B

Pin-prick sized dentine exposed on the maxillary RPm2 and LM2 and mandibular RPm2.

Trench ZJ26, Sp. I

Attrition is seen on deciduous teeth and on erupted 1st permanent molars from maxilla and mandible. The anterior teeth from upper and lower jaw show attrition in between '2 to 3' grades (Fig. 4.27). Attrition pattern for both maxillary and mandibular dm1s, dm2s and M1s is grade '5', grade

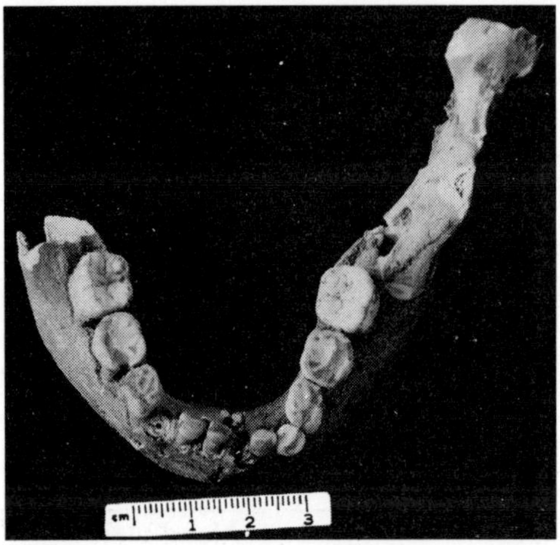

Fig. 4.27 Trench ZJ26, Sp. I: Mandible, occlusal view.

'5' and grade '2', respectively (more precisely, grade of attrition for mandibular RLM1 is in between '1 and 2').

There are some traces of chipping on the maxillary Rdm1 and RLdm2 on the buccal aspect. On Rdm1, some chipping is seen on the buccal side and on Rdm2 on bucco-distal aspect and on mesio-buccal aspect on Ldm2 is evident. The origin of these chipping can be coarse food but the possibility of post-mortem damage cannot be ruled out.

Trench ZJ26, Sp. II

Not much attrition is seen on posterior molar teeth of this individual. From maxilla M1s, M2s and M3s have attrition of grade '5', grade '2' and grade '1', respectively. Mandibular right side molars are preserved in the collection, where M1 exhibits grade '4' attrition, while on M2 and M3 the grade '2' pattern is evident.

Other than attrition, the right canine from maxilla and mandible gives evidence of enamel chipping near the edge on the buccal aspect. Chipping pattern is identical in the upper and lower tooth.

Enamel Hypoplasia

Enamel hypoplasia is a deficiency in enamel thickness due to a disruption during enamel forming activity and is an easily identified marker of stress or growth disruption (Goodman *et al.* 1980). Enamel hypoplasia appears as irregular horizontal linear grooves or pits in the enamel surface, best viewed on the labial (buccal) aspect of the crown.

Microscopic hypoplastic defects provide an indelible and retrospective record of growth disruptive stress occurring during the childhood period (birth to about 13 years) when tooth enamel was being formed and remain as a permanent record into adulthood. Multiple causal factors can produce enamel hypoplasia, including nutritional stress (Hush-Ashmore *et al.* 1982), Vitamin D deficiency and fever. While the specific cause of a particular hypoplastic defect cannot be determined, the mere existence of a defect indicates a stress of sufficient magnitude to disrupt the normal growth process.

Since the chronology of tooth formation is known, the developmental age at which a growth disruption occurred in a child can be precisely determined. Hypoplasias of deciduous or baby teeth represents stress in utero or immediately after birth and, therefore, tends to reflect maternal health and nutrition (Cohen 1989). Multiple hypoplasias in a single individual yield clues to the timing or periodicity of repetitive stresses, such as recurring seasonal scarcity of nutrients. Differences in the frequency of enamel hypoplasias between sexes, social status and groups with different subsistence bases can provide valuable data on the pattern of stress in a prehistoric population (Hush-Ashmore *et al.* 1982).

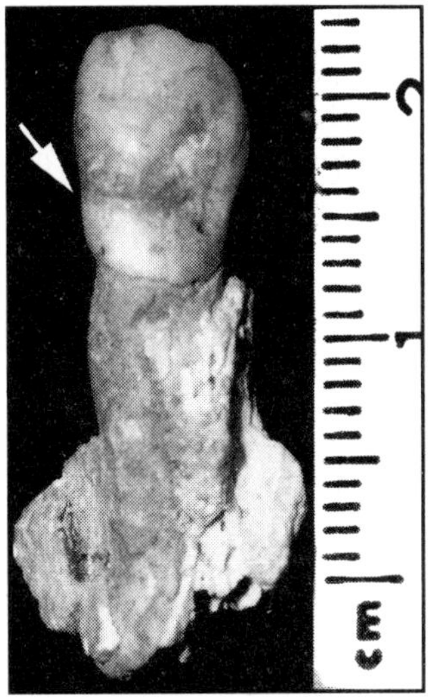

Fig. 4.28 Trench ZJ26, Sp. II: mandibular canine, note the hypoplastic line.

The following method has been adopted while estimating the age of disturbance in case of primary teeth:

a. Status of calcification achieved at birth is the first consideration.
b. Accordingly, from the total crown height, an appropriate measure is subtracted as development before birth.
c. While presuming that the remaining crown developed at a uniform rate, the remaining crown height is taken as development occurred till the crown completion or till the individual died, whichever is earlier.
d. Using the height of lesion from the CEJ, month of disturbance is calculated.

Enamel hypoplastic lesions can appear in three forms: linear enamel hypoplasia, localized enamel hypoplasia and enamel pits. In the Kodumanal dental series, the enamel defects appear in the form of lines, and in one case as pit (Table 4.14). Interestingly, there is a case where age of disturbance is at a very young age. This individual, Meg. I, Sp. III-B, died at the age of 14 + 2 months. The hypoplastic line suggests the age of stress at around 3 months. It may be noted that this individual also gives an evidence of periostosis on the fibula mid-shaft.

Specimen ZJ26, Sp. II, displays hypoplastic line(s) on 10 of its teeth, out of the 20 elements preserved (Fig. 4.28). The most common period of

Table 4.14 Prevalence of Enamel Hypoplasia

Death age	Tooth	Description	Calcification begins	Calcification status at birth	Calcification complete	Crown height	Distance of the lesion from CEJ	Estimated time of disturbance
Meg. I, Specimen III-B								
14 m $\pm$ 2 months	Lower Rdm2	Tooth is unerupted, but the mandibular bone is damaged, permitting inspection of the tooth. The hypoplastic line is not very clear.	6.0 m in utero	Cusps join	10 - 11 m	4.41	3.02	Around 3 months
Meg. X, Specimen B								
18-20 years	Maxillary RM3	Deformed enamel pit of approx. 1 mm, on the mesial aspect of the crown	7-10 y	-	12-16 y	6.77	4.18	Around 10 years
Specimens ZJ26, sp I								
7 $\pm$ 1 year	Maxillary RM1	Hypoplastic pit on the mesio-lingual aspect. Maximum diameter of the pit is 1.56 mm	Birth	-	2.5-3 y	6.68	1.29	Around 2.5 years
	Maxillary RM2	Liner enamel hypoplasia, on the buccal aspect of this incompletely calcified crown	2.5-3 y	-	7-8 y	5.78	2.26	Around 5 years
	Maxillary LM2	Liner enamel hypoplasia, on the buccal aspect of this incompletely calcified crown	2.5-3 y	-	7-8 y	6.16	2.31	Around 5 years

Table 4.14 *contd.*

Death age	Tooth	Description	Calcification begins	Calcification status at birth	Calcification complete	Crown height	Distance of the lesion from CEJ	Estimated time of disturbance
Specimens ZJ26, sp I contd...								
	Mandibular RM2	Liner enamel hypoplasia, on the buccal aspect of this incompletely calcified crown	2.5-3 y	-	7-8 y	5.65	3.74	Around 5 years
Specimens ZJ26, specimen II								
25 ± 5 years	Maxillary LI1	Two faint hypoplastic lines on the labial aspect	3-4 m	-	4-5 y	11.05	1st line: 6.62 2nd line:5.14	2.5 years 3 years
	Maxillary LI2	Hypoplastic line on the buccal side	10-12 m	-	4-5 y	11.21	7.60	3.5 years
	Maxillary LPm2	Faint line of deficient enamel on almost entire crown.	2-2.5 y	-	6-7 y	6.13	2.40	Around 3 years
	Maxillary RM1	One clear line covering entire crown	Birth	-	2.5-3 y	7.42	2.00	2 year
	Maxillary RM3	One faint line covering entire crown	7-10 y	-	12-16 y	7.93	2.16	13 years
	Mandibular RI1	Two faint lines covering entire crown	3-4 m	-	4-5 y	8.18	1st line:4.17 2nd line:3.29	2 years 2.5 years
	Mandibular LI1	Two faint lines covering entire crown	3-4 m	-	4-5 y	9.23	1st line: 3.97 2nd line:3.18	2 years 2.5 years
	Mandibular RI2	Two faint lines covering entire crown	3-4 m	-	4-5 y	10.61	1st line:4.60 2nd line:3.66	3.5 years 4 years
	Mandibular RM1	One faint line only on the buccal aspect	Birth	-	2.5-3 y	6.98	2.85	2.5 year

disturbance is around 2-3 years of age, noted for seven of these teeth. One tooth (mandibular RI2) displays two lines, one of which gives age of disturbance as 3.5 year and the other line as 4 years. Line on maxillary RM3 provides the memory of stress episode occurred when the individual was 13 years old.

For specimen ZJ26, Sp. I, the most common episode of stress appears to be around 4 to 5 years. Out of the four hypoplastic lesions noted, three suggest the stress age at around 5 years, while one lesion refers to the stress occurring at around 2.5 years. This child died at the age of 7 ± 1 year.

For Specimen Meg. X-B, only one tooth shows hypoplastic line, which gives the age at stress of around 10 years.

For the protohistoric populations of the Deccan Plateau, the most common age of stress is noted to be coinciding with the weaning age (Mushrif 2002). Many factors like non-feeding of colostrum, nutritional inadequacy of the weaning food, maternal neglect and culturally imposed food taboos are stated to be responsible for higher morbidity and mortality during the weaning phase. However, in the Kodumanal series, no stress episode of this phase is recorded in the form of deficient enamel. The problems occurring between 2-3 years or at 5 years might not be solely nutritionally originated but appear to be resulting from increased exposure to pathogens.

It may be noted that all available long bones of the immature individuals were x-rayed, but no bone gives evidence of Harris lines.

Tarter Accumulation

Another irritant found in the one of the Kodumanal specimens, Specimen ZJ26, Sp. II, is calculus deposition on dental elements. It is seen on almost all preserved teeth. For the anterior teeth, the deposit is on the buccal surface while for the posterior teeth, the lingual aspect is affected. The teeth affected are maxillary LI1, LI2 and RLC on buccal side, LPm1, RPm2, RM1, RM2 and RM3 on lingual aspect; Mandibular RLI1 on buccal and RPm1, RM1, M2 and M3 on lingual side. There are slight traces of tarter accumulation on the lingual aspect of the anterior teeth as well.

Calculus and its precursor, bacterial plaque, consist of a sticky coating including protein, food particles, living and dead micro-organisms. When plaque mineralises, it becomes calculus and in this form can be found on archaeological skeletal specimens as relatively hard additions to the tooth

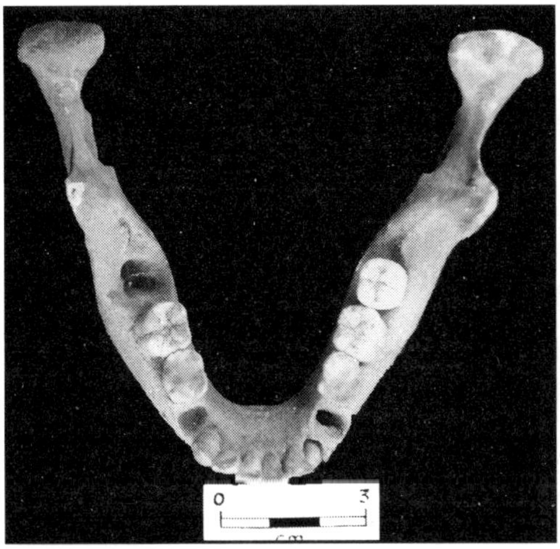

Fig. 4.29 Trench ZJ26, Sp. III: Mandible, occlusal view.

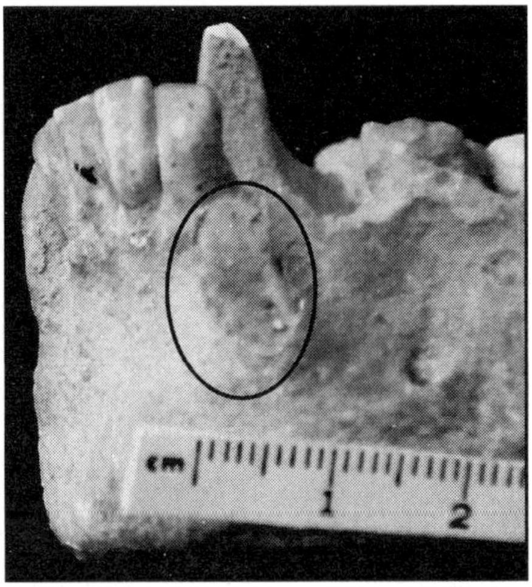

Fig. 4.30 Trench ZJ26, Sp. III: Close-up of un-erupted permanent canine.

surface usually at the margins of the gums (Ortner and Putschar 1984). The role of calculus in periodontal disease is not clear. In any case, the presence of calculus on dental tissues is an important consideration in evaluating the irritation of gum tissue and possible cause of periodontal disease. Calculus deposits are very common in archaeological skeletal material and often they coexist with severe attrition. The occlusal surfaces are usually free from such deposits, but if they are coated, the inference is mal-occlusion of jaws, or perhaps a prolonged illness in which the person's oral health is severely declined.

Dental Asymmetry and Crowding

Among the miscellaneous dental pathologies, noted in this series is dental asymmetry in the eruption process and crowding.

In ZJ26, Sp. III, there is slight bilateral discrepancy in the dental eruption process (Figs. 4.29 and 4.30). It could just be morphological in origin, but possibility of stress cannot be ruled out. Generally, the dental eruption sequence is genetically controlled and does not get much affected with environmental or nutritional stress on the person. For this individual, mandibular right canine is already erupted, while for the left side tooth the eruption process has just started. From maxilla, the RPm1 was erupted (but lost post-mortem). For the left side, Ldm1 has been shed and eruption process for LPm1 appears to have begun. Again, maxillary RPm2 shows

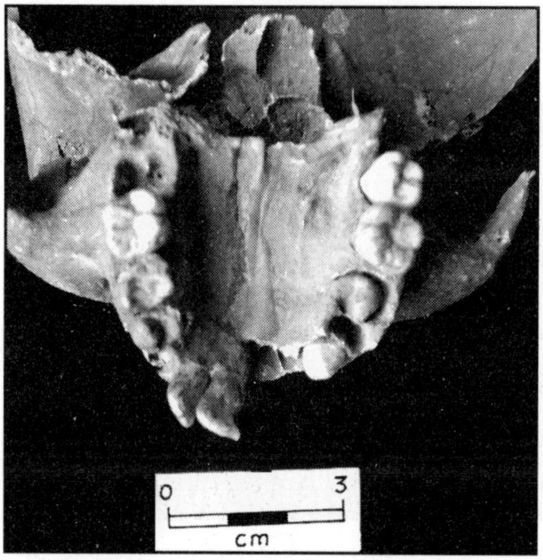

Fig. 4.31 Trench ZJ26, Sp. III: Maxilla, occlusal view, note dental crowding.

beginning state of eruption, while the Ldm2 is still retaining its position in the crypt. Eruption process of LPm2 will begin only after this tooth is lost.

In the same specimen, dental crowding of maxillary anterior teeth is also evident. Dental crowding is seen on the maxillary left first and second incisors (Fig. 4.31), and mandibular right and left second incisor and canine regions (see Fig. 4.29). The right side maxillary incisors are lost post-mortem precluding any kind of observation. This child also has moderate 'overbite' indicating prognathism (see Fig. 3.13).

Although teeth of this child do not give evidence of enamel disturbance, he probably suffered from iron deficiency. Both right and left orbital roofs exhibit *cribra orbitalia* in the form of porosity. All these problems suggest that this child must have suffered from moderate stress and/or nutritional deficiency, which disturbed the eruption process to a certain extent.

Considering these pathologies, it appears that the dental eruption discrepancy might have been pathological in origin.

The etiology of dental crowding is complex and includes both genetic and environmental factors (King 1983). The displacement of teeth from their 'normal' anatomical relationship because of lack of adequate developmental jaw space is called crowding (Lukacs 1989). Crowding tends to occur in certain areas of the dental arcade more than others. Third molar teeth and anterior incisor teeth are more prone to crowding. It is taken as a fairly good indicator of severe stress, either nutritional or endemic acute problems. Under chronic conditions, the alveolar bone size development is more affected. The dental calcification process, on the other hand, is largely genetically controlled. This results in decrease in the space available for each tooth. It has been observed that increased crowding and impacted molars are more common in severely malnourished children

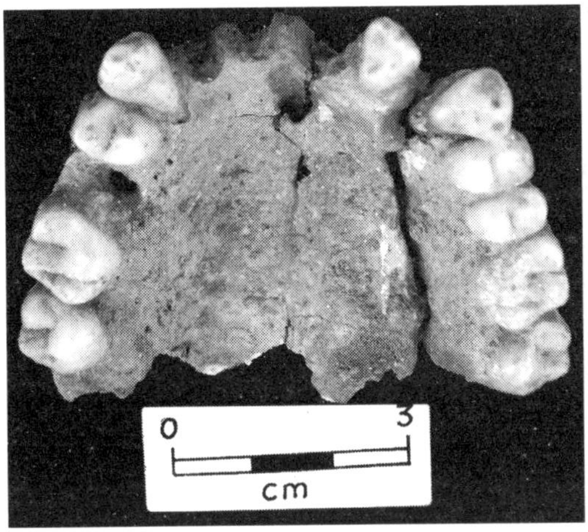

Fig. 4.32 Meg. I, Sp. I: Maxilla, Occlusal view.

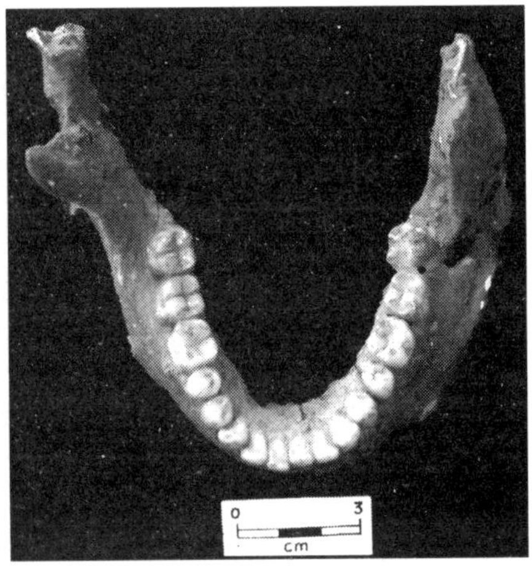

Fig. 4.33 Meg. I, Sp. I: Mandible, Occlusal view.

(Widdowson and McCance 1964). Increasing incidence of this lesion may be indicative of severe and chronic stress in archaeological populations.

If adequate jaw space is available, but the tooth is rotated from proper alignment, this is not considered as crowding. Such rotation of a tooth may occur in normal dentitions. Mesiopalatal rotation of maxillary central incisors, dental winging (Dahlberg and Enoki 1958), is often recorded as a dental morphological variant.

It may also be noted that greater dental asymmetry, such as size differences in right and left counterparts, differences on morphological features, asymmetrical rotation, etc. are found to be correlated with physiological stress (Bailit *et al.* 1970). Though the causative mechanism is not clearly understood yet, it is suggested that the disturbances during the prenatal life are likely to be more critical.

D. Age-Sex Estimation

I. Age Estimation

Meg. I, Sp. I

This individual was studied by Reddy and Reddy (1987). On the basis of the teeth eruption and wear (Fig. 4.32 and 4.33), fusion of epiphyses of the long bones and condition of the cranial sutures, they conclude death age for this individual as 'not more than 35 years'. The present authors agree with the said age estimation for this individual.

Meg. I, Sp. II

This specimen was also studied earlier by Reddy and Reddy (1987). They comment that "(this individual) seems to have faced death before attaining the age of 30 years as could be seen from the condition of the teeth, epiphyses of bones, etc." The present authors prefer to put the age range for this individual as 'around 30 years' at the time of death.

Meg. I, Sp. III-A

Very few bones are preserved for this individual. On the basis of morphological scrutiny of the few bones of cranial cap and small bone fragments, the earlier scholars (Reddy and Reddy 1987) conclude that "the specimen is undoubtedly that of a child of not more than 6 years of age when it died as could be seen from the condition of the cranial parts". The present authors also agree with the age estimation.

Meg. I, Sp. III-B

Very few bones represent this individual. One tooth, Rdm2, and one long bone preserved provide some clues for estimating age at the time of death. The Rdm2 is in crypt but has almost complete crown calcification. Usually the crown calcification for this tooth is complete between the 10th to 11th month. The preserved long bone L radius gives height estimation of 85 mm. Normal growth rate seen among infants and early children of the peninsular protohistoric populations is stated to be around 90 to 85 per cent of the standard (Walimbe-Gambhir 1984). Using the same standard and by judging of the crown development of dm2, this individual could be placed in the range of '14 m $\pm$ 2 months' at the time of death.

Meg. IV

For this individual, age estimation is based on cranial morphology and dentition. On the basis of overall morphology, this individual is a full grown adult. Third molars from upper (RM3) and lower jaws (RM3) are erupted. The eruption of the third molar generally occurs between 18-20 years. These molars were fully erupted and were being used as is evident from the negligible amount of attrition seen. The first and second molars from upper and lower jaws are moderately worn showing 'grade 5' and 'grade 4', respectively. On the basis of the wear pattern, this individual was probably between 25 to 30 years old at the time of death.

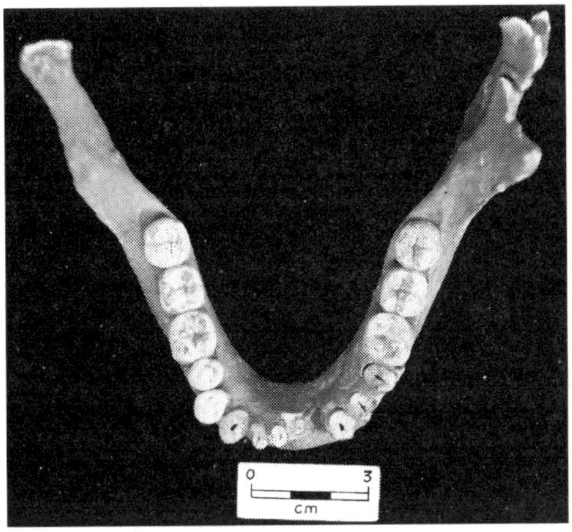

Fig. 4.34 Meg. IX- A: Mandible, occlusal view.

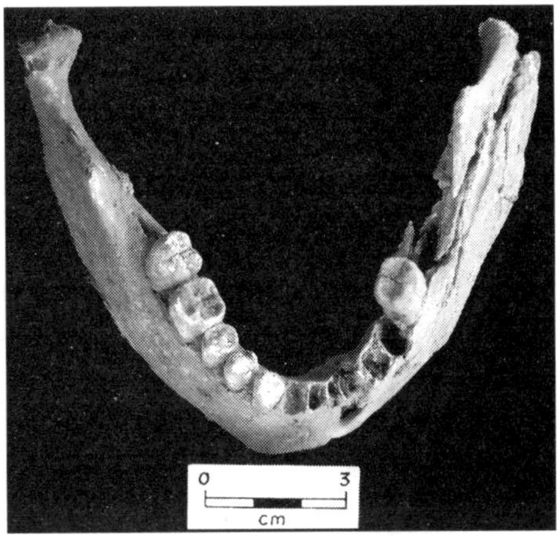

Fig. 4.35 Meg. IX-B: Mandible, occlusal view.

Meg. V

The skeletal elements are in fragmentary condition. Yet, on the basis of overall morphological observation and dental attrition pattern, a rough age estimate of 'around 30 years' can be given for this 'middle-aged adult' individual.

Meg. IX-A

Death age for this young adult is difficult to estimate since it is to be based only on the dental wear pattern. The third molar is erupted and shows negligible amount of attrition. Even the first and second molars of upper and lower jaws exhibit less amount of attrition (Fig. 4.34). This indicates that the age of this individual was around 25 years at the time of death.

Meg. IX-B

Age estimation is based on the eruption of third molar and the attrition pattern seen on dentition. Though the third molar of this individual is not erupted, the overall morphology suggests adult status of this individual. Probably, the third molar was not erupted. On the basis of 'Standard' (Buikstra and Ubelaker 1994), the wear pattern for the maxillary first and second molars is in between 'grade 1 and 2'. The mandibular molar RM1 is more worn showing 'grade 4' attrition pattern (Fig. 4.35). On the basis of the wear pattern and general skeletal features, it may be concluded that this individual was a 'young adult', may be around 18 to 20 years of age when he died.

Meg. X-A

Both maxillary third molars are erupted and in occlusal level. Moderate attrition is seen on the mandibular RLM1 and not much wear is evident on RLM2. On the basis of this observation and general skeletal features, this individual was probably around 25 years old at the time of death.

Meg. X-B

Age of this specimen is based on overall morphology and very few preserved teeth. Both mandibular RLM1 are present which do not show any attrition. Maxillary LM2 also has no wear on the occlusal surface. This indicates that this specimen was very young at the time of death. On the basis of these observations, the individual can be placed in the age range of '18 to 20 years', more likely to be 'around 18 years'.

Trench ZJ26, Sp. I

This is a sub-adult individual. Upper and lower first permanent molars are erupted, which usually erupt between 6-7 years of age. Permanent RI1 and RI2 shows complete crown calcification and the beginning of the root calcification. Usually, the crowns of central and lateral incisors complete the calcification process between 4 to 5 years, which confirms that the child was not less than 5 years at the time of death. The maxillary RLM2 and Mandibular RM2 exhibit almost complete calcified crown, which usually completes between 7-8 years, indicating that the child was not more that 8 year old.

Long bone diaphyseal lengths can also be used to estimate the age of this child. Four long bones are available for length measurement, L humerus (17 cm), R radius (13.07 cm), L ulna (14.05 cm), and R femur (25 cm). These measurements when compared with the modern reference skeletons of known age, suggest an age of around 7 years for this individual.

Comparing both dental as well as long bone lengths, the child can be placed 'around 7 $\pm$ 1 year' bracket.

Trench ZJ26, Sp. II

This is an adult individual. The maxillary and mandibular third molars are erupted and they were in use at the time of death. Slight wear is seen on these molars (grade 1). The wear pattern on first and second maxillary molars (grade 5 and 2, respectively) indicates the death age of the specimen as around 25 ± 5 years.

Trench ZJ26, Sp. III

Age estimation of this individual is based on dental eruption sequence and long bone length measurements as well as on overall morphology.

All permanent second molars (maxillary M2 and mandibular M2) are erupted. Generally, second molars erupt around the age between 12-13 years. In case of premolars, the RPm1 from maxilla and RLPm1 from mandible were erupted, an event which usually happens around 11 to 12 years. There is every possibility that the eruption process of RPm2 was started before the individual died, as the Rdm2 was already fallen. The eruption of Pm2 happens in between 10 to 12 years. This indicates that the child was more than 12 years old.

The general morphology of the child shows little older age. Preserved three long bones give length measurements as R ulna: 18.50 cm, L radius: 17.00 cm, and L tibia: 21.00 cm. Comparing this data with reference skeletons give an age of around 13 years.

It may be concluded that the individual was between 12 to 13 years of age at the time of death.

Estimation of age at death for the two *"miscellaneous"* individuals is as follows: It may be noted that since archaeological association of these remains is not precisely known, the age inferences are not of any significance while drawing demographic profile for the Kodumanal series.

Misc. 1: This specimen is represented by very few bones. From the upper extremity, only the right humerus fragment has preserved, while RL tibia (R almost complete but extremities damaged, L more than 3/4th, 1/4th from distal side broken) represents the lower extremity. These bones are sturdy and strong. Right side tibia provides length measurement (14 cm), which when compared with the skeletal growth charts for the contemporary populations (Walimbe and Gambhir 1994) indicates the age of about 28 months for this individual at the time of death.

Misc. 2: Just two permanent mandibular teeth (LI2 and LC) represent this individual. It is difficult to ascertain the age of this individual. The permanent canine is erupted suggesting the age not less than 12 years. At the same times, both the teeth show slight wear, indicating that teeth were in use for some time before the individual died. In the absence of any other skeletal representation, a rough death age of around 15 years may be suggested.

II. Sex Determination

Out of the 15 individuals identified from the Kodumanal skeletal series, sex determination is possible for nine specimens. The remaining six individuals are sub-adults, and consequently the secondary sex characteristics have not been manifested in them. While standard methodology (Buikstra and Ubelaker 1994) has been used while grading the cranial features and morphology of the sciatic notch, for individuals having poor or no preservation of these parts the sex judgement is based on general morphological observations.

Meg. I, Sp. I

The earlier scholars and present authors conclude the sex of this specimen as male. Reddy and Reddy (1987) base their comment on "anatomical features as highly developed supra orbital ridges, muscular impressions of the nuchal region, highly developed mastoid processes and robust bones and big teeth in its skull and narrow and deeper sciatic notch in its pelvis" (pp. 103).

Meg. I, Sp. II

This individual is stated to be a female, as Reddy and Reddy (1987) remark ".....in view of the moderately developed superciliary arches, weak muscular impressions on the nuchal regions and moderately developed mastoid processes and relatively thicker (?) cranial bones than in specimen 1, and pelvis with wider and shallow sciatic notch" (pp. 103). The cranial elements were not available for study to the present authors.

Meg. I, Sp. III-A

Sex determination is not possible because of sub-adult status of this individual.

Meg. I, Sp. III-B

Sex determination is not possible due to sub-adult status of this individual.

Meg. IV

It is difficult to ascertain the sex of this individual for two reasons. First, the skeletal preservation is very poor, and secondly, no sexually diagnostic part is present in the collection. On the basis of general morphological assessment, the preserved cranial fragments appear to be considerably robust. Tentatively, therefore, sex of this individual is identified as male.

Meg. V

For this individual also, precise sex determination is not possible. The preserved elements are fragmentary and no sexually diagnostic part is present in the collection. The robustness of linea aspera and the fibular fragment can be used to tentatively ascribe male sex to this individual.

Meg. IX-A

No bones from pelvic region are preserved for this individual. But sexually diagnostic features on skull are available for inspection. General robust morphology of the specimen indicates the male sex for this specimen. The mastoid process can be graded in between '4 and 5'. The supraorbital margin is of 'grade 4'. This confirms the male sex of this individual.

Meg. IX-B

In this case, the pelvis fragment with partially preserved greater sciatic notch is the main criteria for sex determination. The angle of the sciatic notch is of 'grade 1', which is typical of female pelvis. As mentioned earlier, there were two individuals in the burial pit and they were mixed together. The association of this pelvis fragment with the said individual is based on the general gracile morphology of the skeletal remains. In comparison with other male individuals (Meg. IX-A) from the same burial, this individual is gracile in nature, which is indicative of female sex.

Meg. X-A

For this individual, the pelvis fragment with greater sciatic notch is preserved in the collection. The angel of sciatic notch is of 'grade 4', which confirms male sex of this specimen. The overall robusticity also indicates male sex for this individual.

Meg. X-B

The preservation of this individual is very fragmentary and no part from pelvis or cranium is present for sex determination. Only on the basis of the overall gracile appearance of skeletal elements, the individual is taken as female. Another individual from the same burial (Meg. X-A) is identified as male, and in comparison with this specimen (Meg. X-B) is gracile, which is taken as indicative of a female sex. It must also be noted that the right side human distal extremity present in the collection gives an evidence of a foramen in the olecranon fossa. This fossa is more commonly observed in females (Bass 1981).

Trench ZJ26, Sp. I

Sex determination is not possible due to sub-adult status of this individual.

Trench ZJ26, Sp. II

The overall cranial and post-cranial features show robustness. The heftiness is evident in the glabellar fragment, mastoid process and occipital protuberance. Long bones like femur and tibia show muscular marking areas. The confirmation of the male sex of this individual comes on the basis of preserved angle of right sciatic notch of 'grade 4', which is taken as typical of male type.

Trench ZJ26, Sp. III

Sex determination is not possible due to the sub-adult status of this individual.

Misc. I: Sex determination is not possible due to the sub-adult status of this individual.

Misc. II: Sex determination is not possible due to the sub-adult status of this individual.

Table 4.15 Summary of the age estimation and sex determination for the entire series

Specimen no.	Sex	Age
Meg. I, Sp. I	Male	30 to 35 years
Meg. I, Sp. II	Female	Around 30 years
Meg. I, Sp. III-A	Undetermined	5 to 6 years
Meg. I, Sp. III-B	Undetermined	14 ± 2 months
Meg. IV	Male	25 to 30 years
Meg. V	Male?	Around 30 years
Meg. IX-A	Male	Around 25 years
Meg. IX-B	Female	18 to 20 years
Meg. X-A	Male	Around 25 years
Meg. X-B	Female	18 to 20 years
Trench ZJ26, Sp. I	Undetermined	6 to 7 years
Trench ZJ26, Sp. II	Male	30 ± 5 years
Near Tr. ZJ26, Sp. III	Undetermined	11 to 12 years
Misc	Undetermined	28 months
Misc	Undetermined	Around 15 years
Specimen housed at Madras	Not attempted	Not attempted

NOTES AND REFERENCES

1. In certain cases, published literature does not give the MCA figures (for example, the publications for Bellan Bandi Palassa, Langhnaj, Rupar, Burzahom). The present authors have calculated these figures by multiplying the given mean values of mesio-distal and bucco-lingual diameter.

5

Concluding Remarks

The report on the Kodumanal human skeletal series is important in many ways. The site of Kodumanal is one of the best excavated, best attended, and best reported Megalithic-Early Historic sites of the peninsular region. The skeletal remains were in fairly good state of preservation, and more importantly made available for detailed anthropological study. The report deviates from the conventional anthropological design, but follows the bio-cultural approach which provides information on many important facets of this bygone population.

The traditional approach in human skeletal biology had aimed to classify the populations on the basis of their phenotypic features, like physical characterizations like face or head shape. More seriously, in archaeological context, *'racial'* similarities or differences in two skeletal populations were used to emphasize either cultural contact or changes in the material culture (for example, Sewell and Guha 1931; Guha and Basu 1938). This was the trend of the early 20th century when theories of invasion, migration and 'mixing of blood' were the answers to diversities or 'discrepancies' noted in the skeletal record. In other words, anthropological research was guided by archaeological needs and the anthropological evidence was used primarily to complement archaeological hypotheses of cultural migration or diffusion. This approach, which was descriptive and limited to racial classification, was inadequate to deal with the questions related to human adaptation. Gradually, anthropologists began to take the skeletal variations as the net result of a highly complex process of genetic and non-genetic factors. This conceptual change necessitated re-evaluation of the skeletal data and the earlier hypotheses needed to be reframed. The techniques employed for racial categorization continued, with better standardization, but the findings no longer constituted a mere appendix to the archaeological reports. Now skeletal remains are looked not as isolated pieces of evidence, but by placing the skeletal material into an assigned cultural context, anthropologists try to better understand the ability of the humans to adapt to new environments by adopting appropriate cultural strategies and responding biologically within the plausible phenotypic range, as determined by genotype. This also helped trace the evolutionary routes of the human form in time and also to establish the movement of populations from different areas with improvements in technology.

Research on archaeological human skeletal remains was negligible in India till the 1950s. Though more attention is being paid now, conditions are far from being satisfactory even today. Excavation reports for more than 350 sites record the existence of human burials (Kennedy and Caldwell 1984, Walimbe and Tavares 2002). However, skeletal material has been neatly attended anthropologically only from about 40 sites. Evidence recovered from other sites is either lost forever or still awaits careful anthropological scrutiny. The reasons for overlooking human skeletal evidence are many. The general lack of awareness regarding the research potential of the data on the part of many excavators was, and continues to be, one of the major reasons for the slow progress of the discipline in India. While the archaeological evidence of burial was always sought for, since physical anthropologists were very rarely involved in actual excavations, no adequate post-excavation care was rendered to the bones. In many cases, fragmentary bones were often overlooked or not meticulously collected in the field. Many of the excavators never bothered to have their collections studied by the experts. The case of Kodumanal is welcome exception in this regard.

As stated earlier, until the early 1980s human skeletal studies were primarily focused to answer specific questions pertaining to establishing the *'ethnic'* or *'racial'* identity of the concerned population (see Kennedy, 2000). Studies on the Megalithic skeletal series were designed on similar research model. The present authors categorically prefer not to ascribe any *'racial'* label to the Kodumanal population. But a general comment summarizing the studies may be useful.

During the 1930s, general contention was that "the Megalithic cultural complex had been imported to peninsular India from outside by Dravidian-speaking acculturators who imposed their language and certain racial traits upon the non-Dravidian-speaking aboriginals" (*cited from* Kennedy 1975:39). The skeletal studies drew their inferences primarily from the craniometric features, and more specifically cranial index was the main diagnostic criteria. With regard to the Megalithic population in India, specimens from Adichchanallur, Ramgarh, Sanur, Ranchi, Savandurga and Pomparippu are represented by the dolichocranic head form, whereas specimens from Brahmagiri, Nagarjunakonda and Yelleswaram represent the brachycranic head form. These two categories have often led writers to assume that the specimens from the latter group of sites belong to an 'intruder population' replacing the earlier dolichocranic Neolithic inhabitants of the area. On the basis of studies carried out on Brahmagiri and Maski skeletal series, Sarkar (1972) claimed that the Megalithic population belonged to a single racial stock. Homogeneity of Megalithic builders of Brahmagiri and Maski as members of a single race instigated him, like many scholars of earlier generation, as to identify them as "a new wave of people" coming to India. The cradle of origin was usually set in the Meditterranean region (Childe 1947, Sarkar 1972) or in the Southeast Asia (Furer-Haimendorf 1945, Zuckerman 1930). The existence of cairn burials, which typify the Megalithic culture in North India and among some of the living tribal populations, also doubted the 'sudden invasion' of new people. It does, however, seem unscientific to assume that a broad-headed population arriving from outside the continent suddenly uprooted an aboriginal dolichocranic population. Brachycrany is encountered, though in smaller proportions, in the skeletal record from several Harappan and Neolithic-Chalcolithic sites (Walimbe and Tavares 2002). It is an established fact that the terminal Pleistocene population groups underwent an evolutionary process, resulting in gradual increase in brachycrany over dolichocrany, though some people retained their dolichocranic feature. Though genetic influences in determining a regional phenotype cannot be ignored completely, changes in cranio-facial morphology have been attributed to non-genetic factors, the most important of which is the food preparation technique. The differential functional demands on the body (inclusive of more sophisticated food preparation techniques), and increased nutritional stress are stated to be the main factors influencing cranio-facial morphological changes among the early farming societies. The most noticeable changes are decrease in cranial length, increase in cranial height, smaller dentition, rotation of the facial region to a position more inferior to the cranium, straight or orthognathous face, and progressive decrease in robusticity (Walimbe 1998). These changes are very well documented in the Kodumanal series.

Coming back to the hypothesis of phenotypic homogeneity of the Indian Iron Age populations, Kennedy (1975) had re-examined the skeletal collections from the sites mentioned above and also from other sites, including Raigir, Ramgarh, Ranchi, Sanur and Nagarjunakonda. Rigorous multivariate analysis of the data led to the conclusion that variability of physical characteristics is a conspicuous feature of the biological nature of the Megalithic population (Kennedy 1975, Kennedy and Levisky 1984). This study made it clear that no single character typified the Megalithic populations, least of all variations in cranial form, thus rejecting Sarkar's claim that brachycrany was the hallmark of the Megalithic builders of Brahmagiri and Maski. Nor did this study support the thesis of a catastrophic invasion of foreign people into the southern Deccan with the introduction of iron technology, as Wheeler had proposed, and indicated a biological continuum of Neolithic-Chalcolithic populations to Iron Age population (Kennedy 2000). In a way, this inference corroborates the author's claim of indigenous evolutionary development of morphological features, induced by non-biological factors (Walimbe 2007).

The issue of biological continuity from the Neolithic-Chalcolithic populations can better be studied using morphological features than metric features. Metric features are more adaptive in nature. On the other hand, morphological traits are not only having low susceptibility to environmental change, but also show little to no sexual dimorphism, and lack age-related changes; thus permit using sub-adult and fragmentary skeletal/dental remains in comparative studies which are otherwise useless in metric studies. Therefore, in comparison with the studies based on continuous traits, non-metric cranial discrete traits and dental occlusal morphological features appear more accurate for understanding population distances, and to infer past population relationships and movements. A study by Hawkey (2002) on 29 dental morphological features using a large sample size of more than 4000 teeth is the most comprehensive account in this line of research. This study also supports the hypothesis of indigenous development of Iron Age Megalith builders. "The dental morphological data further indicates that there is little evidence to support an external origin for the Iron Age / Megalithic populations. The data rather suggest the origins of the Iron Age populations within central and southern peninsular India, and not from north-western regions... The populations, however, maintain affinity with the farming-herding groups of the Deccan" (Hawkey 2002:195).

To summarise, it may be stated that no single phenotype characterizes the Megalithic population but variability of physical characteristics is seen prominently. The variability is because of the biological continuum of local Neolithic-Chalcolithic populations to Iron Age population. There is no biological proof to support invasion of foreign people into the southern Deccan with the introduction of iron technology.

The other important facet of this report is detailed palaeopathological scrutiny of the skeletal and dental elements. Palaeodemographic interpretations offered for a skeletal series including estimation of population size, density, mortality and fertility rates, and life expectancy are useful while understanding life ways. Palaeopathological investigations, besides identifying diseases, contribute for better understanding of prehistoric social organization. Differences in status, rank and occupation are expected to have effects on health and nutrition of people because of differential access to the food resources. These health and dietary differences are reflected in the bones and can be read in archaeological populations.

Demographic features of the protohistoric inhabitants of the peninsula have been speculated in detail (for detailed bibliography, see Walimbe and Tavares 2002). The most significant finding of this research is high infant mortality rates, estimated to be as high as 45-50 per cent. The high mortality of the early agricultural populations is attributed to the physiological stress resulting from excessive population pressure, under- and/or mal-nourishment and infections. These factors played a vital role in controlling the demographic set-up of the population at least in the initial agricultural phase, a phenomenon observed world-wide in many populations experiencing changes towards agriculture (Cohen and Armelagos 1984). If the hypothesis of agricultural-based economy holds true for the Megalithic phase, then similar physiological stress might have affected the Megalithic populations as well.

Optimum life expectancy for the Indian Protohistoric populations was around 30 to 35 years (Walimbe and Tavares 2002). Even in Kodumanal series, there is no individual which can be convincingly put under the 'old-adult' age category. At the same time, the paucity of sub-adult segment in the Megalithic series is puzzling. In the Vidarbha Megalithic context, it is possible that immature bone did not survive the destructive pressure of the overlying earth. However, delicate nature of the bones does not explain the enigmatic under-representation of sub-adults, especially when the site of Raipur has yielded a few bones of a two-year-old child (Walimbe 1993). Remains of four sub-adults each from the Kodumanal and Mahurjhari are also worth mentioning in this regard. The Kodumanal series includes remains of an infant of around 14 months, a child of around 28 months and two children between 5 to 7 years of age. For under-representation of sub-adults, the plausible and most likely explanation can be some alternate mode of disposing the dead. Moreover, the site like Kodumanal is spread over 50 acres of habitation and around 100 acres of cemetery yielding 150 graves. Even though the excavated area is not more than 1 per cent, the recovery of 'individuals' is far less than the actual deaths that might have occurred at the site during the 300 to 400 years of occupation. The minimal representation of the graves and the size of the graves and elite nature of grave goods suggest that the elaborate mode of disposal of the dead was not accorded to every individual, but only for elite people. In support of this view, it would be interesting to note that the recent discovery of Tamil-Brahmi inscribed memorial stones found at Thathappatti and Pulimankombi (Dist. Dindugul, Tamil Nadu) and many literary references found in Sangam literature (*Akananuru* 35, 67, 91, 109, 131, 151, 157, 215, 231, 289; *Purananuru* 3, 221, 261, 264, 265, 329) clearly state that the chamber tombs were generally raised for the heroes who died for the welfare of the society (Rajan 2007a, 2007b). Limited occurrence of graves may be attributed to this cultural factor.

Palaeopathological data is meagre for the Iron Age Megalithic or the Early Historic populations. It is clear that the pattern of disease or injury that affects any group of people is never a matter of chance. It is not only the expression of stresses to which they were exposed but also reflects their genetic inheritance, the climate in which they lived, the soil that gave them sustenance and the animals or plants around. Their daily occupation, dietary habits, their choice of dwellings and clothes, their social structure and even their customs influence their morbidity pattern.

On the whole, the Early Historic-Megalithic skeletons are devoid of any significant major infectious pathology. There are a couple of cases of treponematosis, but the diagnosis has been questioned (Rao *et al.* 1996, Baker and Armelagos 1988; Livingstone 1991, Kennedy 2000). Major non-specific infections and nutritional deficiencies observed in these populations include periostitis, porotic hyperostosis and anaemia (Walimbe *in press-b*). Iron deficiency or Vitamin C deficiency is not a disease by itself, but a symptom making the individual prone to catch recurrent infection. At the same time, infections or prolonged illness may lead to anaemic condition. Besides broad range of pathogens, several sociological aspects are important while interpreting these pathologies. Pregnancies at an early age, less child spacing, prolonged lactation and nutritional stress are important aspects to consider while explaining lesions on female specimens.

No major traumatic lesion is noticed in the Kodumanal series. But the evidence from other contemporary sites of the region is worth recording here. A lesion exhibited on the lone adult male skull recovered from the habitation-cum-burial site of S. Pappinayakkanpatti exhibits an extensive scar of wound injury, most probably caused by a sharp and flat metal weapon, such as sword or axe (Walimbe and Selvakumar 1998). Despite the deep injury penetrating the soft tissue of the brain, death was not instantaneous. On the basis of close observation of the damaged bone, it is inferred that the victim survived for some period, anywhere between fifteen days to three months, after the incident. Probably, the complications of post-traumatic infections were more serious considering the openness of the wound. Yet, since the individual survived for a few days after the injury, it is indeed noteworthy that the Iron Age populations had the knowledge and skill to treat such serious injuries.

There are a few interesting incidences of occupational-related infections in the Kodumanal series itself.

Three adult specimens (2 males and a female) of the Kodumanal skeletal series exhibit the lesion of maxillary sinusitis, the possible route of which can be airborne infection. The appearance of infection on female specimen can be attributed to smoke inhalation for cooking in closed walls. Similar incidences have been noted in the early agro-pastoral communities of the Deccan Plateau (Mushrif and Walimbe 2006). Ethnoarchaeological studies documenting air pollution level in the kitchen while cooking are supportive of this conclusion (Reddy 2002).

The pathology in male specimens is more interesting. The lesion could be airborne, and occupation related. The Iron Age and early Historic-Megalithic population of Kodumanal had been engaged in iron smelting and tool making. Though direct co-relation cannot be established, smoke from the iron furnace can be taken as a probable cause. This interpretation gains support when other bones of this specimen are examined. For example, the clavicles of one of the individuals are bilaterally asymmetrical.

The bilateral differences in robusticity and dimensions are occupation related, cased by repetitive movements of certain body parts. More specifically, use of one arm repeatedly for blowing air to furnace or shaping of tools by hammering may induce such morphological changes. Therefore, the authors believe clavicular changes and deformed maxillary floor in the same individual are more likely occupation-related pathologies than mere co-incidental.

There are a few old-age related pathologies reported for the Megalithic populations. The important lesions include osteoarthritis, vertebral osteophytosis (vertebral lipping), etc.

There has always been a controversy regarding the subsistence economy of the Iron Age settlers, whether or not they practiced agriculture. With the exception of a few Iron Age sites which have yielded cultural remains from habitation areas (like Maski, Hallur, Kunnatur, Peddamarur, Kodumanal, Paiyampal-li, Takalghat, Raipur, Mahurjhari, Bhagimohari), it has been impossible to ascertain the dietary patterns of this cultural stage. Though the recent excavations at Mahurjhari have yielded agri-cultural evidence (Mohanty 2005), skeletal and dental pathology were so far the only indirect method of assessing the diet and subsistence pattern for the inhabitants of this Iron Age settlement. Studies on Mahurjhari dentition have suggested a mixed economy (Lukacs 1981). Based on the 'tooth reduction hypothesis', the dental size of Mahurjhari population falls in line with the Mesolithic site of Mahadaha and the Chalcolithic site of Inamgaon, whereas Sarai Khola, an Iron Age site in northern Pakistan, reflects smaller tooth size (Lukacs *et al.* 1989). The site of Sarai Khola is located near the Indus flood plain where agricultural subsistence practices are said to have a much greater antiquity than in Peninsular India (Hemphill *et al.* 1991). Smaller teeth of Kodumanal than many of the megalithic sites could be because of their greater dependence on agriculture and use of sophisticated implements for food preparation. The statement gains support in view of the rich cultural artefacts recovered from the site, reflecting the elegant lifestyle of their possessors. Further, the recovery of paddy from four-legged jars placed as grave goods in a transepted cist at Porunthal in Dindugul district of Tamil Nadu, not far from Kodumanal, yielded clear evidence on the existence of paddy cultivation (Rajan 2009). The less masticatory stress might have acted as a selective force for influencing biology.

Also, intensification of agriculture probably caused certain dental pathologies. Agriculture-based communities are said to exhibit a high prevalence of dental caries, enamel hypoplasia, dental calculus, pulp exposure, dental crowding and alveolar resorption. It is noteworthy that Kodumanal dental series comprises healthy teeth. No infectious diseases, like caries or periodontal lesions, are recorded.

The discipline of skeletal biology like any other developing disciplines has undergone the descriptive and classificatory stages of development. The earlier approach of classifying the populations '*racially*' on the basis of their bodily features is no longer considered adequate to understand the variations evident in skeletal remains and to trace the progress of human evolution and adaptation. Recently adapted 'biocultural perspective' in the analyses of skeletal populations enables the researchers to evaluate populations within their environmental settings and the effects of human activities on the environment. Processes in biology like adaptation, growth, nutrition and their effects on dry bones were utilized to solve and explain the cultural changes that past populations underwent. Previously, palaeoanthropological research was focused only on complete adult crania, since the primary objective of such studies was only to draw conclusions regarding the possible ethnic identity of the population. Infant and sub-adult bones were usually discarded, so also were the post-cranial bones, as these elements do not possess racially diagnostic features. The immediate impact of the changed research perspective is the inclusion of immature and fragmentary bones in the anthropological scrutiny. A significant component of the protohistoric human skeletal series in the Indian subcontinent constitutes sub-adult segment, a condition not very common in the other parts of the world. The finding of sub-adults, belonging to a well-knit temporal, cultural and regional zone, is a definite advantage to biocultural studies in India. Children in the growing age group are more sensitive to any adverse genetic, nutritional, epidemiological, environmental factors and metabolic upsets, in general. Researchers have now realized the potential of sub-adult skeletons, since an individual's history of illness in the delicate period can be read more easily in sub-adults than in mature adult bones, and can be taken as a sensitive indicator to record the effects of subsistence change. There is a long way to go. Many skeletal series must be attended with the new theoretical frame of research, and the study of Kodumanal proves the potential of this approach once again.

A number of techniques have emerged during the last two decades to help skeletal biologists in testing propositions and hypotheses about the relative quality of hunter-gatherer's and farmer's health and nutrition, and more specifically, the effects of an increase in the population densities and less nutritious diet of the farmers as compared to that of the hunter-gatherers. Essentially, osteological studies now demand a multidisciplinary approach and seek help from other physical sciences. Advanced macroscopic and microscopic analysis (SEM) of the bone has contributed a lot to the understanding of lesions and the complexity of human adaptation. Radiographs and photographs of bone are non-destructive ways of analysing bones. Chemical analysis on dry bone has provided new insights into the dynamics of bone tissue in health, disease and nutrition. Trace element and isotopic analysis have forwarded a better understanding of skeletal pathologies not visible by gross analysis. The most investigated and studied has been the Strontium-Calcium ratio, which highlights the cereal versus meat intake by humans. The Sr/Ca ratio has also supplied information on the pattern of dietary supplementation and age of weaning of infants. Change in the weaning age is said to indicate a shift in the subsistence base and is also important to project estimates for population growth rate. Significant boon in the subject is expected from the advances in molecular biology, specially sequencing of mitochondrial DNA, for understanding the process of peopling of India from the protohistoric times.

Though interpretive phase in the discipline has already commenced, there is a long way to go. National level efforts are required to overcome its serious lacunae and drawbacks. For example, proper co-ordination in various anthropology/archaeology museums and excavating agencies would help create a good database of archaeological human skeletal material, which is the prerequisite for research on skeletal biology. The subject demands a more intimate interaction between archaeologists and skeletal biologists. The osseous remains should be collected with great care: not only should adult crania be recorded but every post-cranial and sub-adult or infant bone, fragmentary or complete, should be adequately attended to and be made available to skeletal biologists. Since physical anthropologists rarely participate in excavations, adequate care is not given to delicate pathological bones. Since such bones are often fragmentary, they are often overlooked or not meticulously collected in the field. Similarly, interaction between medical practitioners and palaeopathologists is expected. There is a lack of clinical database with a good cross-section of the population of a particular region and community.

Lack of adequate training facilities, limited exposure of students to the skeletal remains and inadequate literature limit the growth of this interesting field of research in the subcontinent.

The Indian skeletal record, covering a vast time span, can be used to carry out meaningful research and would help skeletal biologists as well as archaeologists to understand the interaction between ancient populations and their habitats, the shift from a hunting-gathering lifestyle to a settled way of life. The subject of human skeletal biology has come a long way from the classification of the fossils of 'ancient man' and grouping them into 'ethnic classes' to studying the skeletal record as an entity in itself, which has a wide scope for providing answers regarding the continuous biocultural adaptation of ancient populations of the subcontinent.

Bibliography

Ayer, A.A. 1960. Report on Human Remains Excavated at Piklihal Near Mudgal, in *Piklihal Excavations* (F.R. Allchin, ed.), pp. 143-154. Hyderabad: Andhra Pradesh Government Archaeological series.

Bailit, H., P.L.Workman, J.K. Niswander and C.J. MacClean. 1970. Dental Asymmetry as an Indicator of Genetic and Environmental Stress in Human Populations, *Human Biology* 42: 626-638.

Baker, B.J. and G.J. Armelagos. 1988. The Origin and Antiquity of Syphilis: Palaeopathological Diagnosis and Interpretation, *Current Anthropology* 29: 703-737.

Bass, W.M. 1881. *Human Osteology: A Laboratory and Field Manual of the Human Skeleton*. 2nd Ed. Missouri: University of Missouri.

Baynes, R.D. and T.H. Brothwell. 1990. Iron Deficiency, *Annual Review of Nutrition* 10: 133-148.

Brothwell, D.R. 1981. *Digging of Bones*. London: British Museum.

Buikstra, J.E. and D.H. Ubelaker. 1994. *Standards for Data Collection from Human Skeletal Remains*. Arkansas: Arkansas Archaeological Survey Research Series, No. 44.

Chatterjee, B.K. and P. Gupta. 1963. *Report on the Adittanalur Skulls*. Calcutta: Anthropological Survey of India.

Childe, V.G. 1947. Megaliths, *Ancient India* 4: 5-13.

Cohen, M.N. 1989. *Health and the Rise of Civilization*. New York: Yale University Press.

Cohen, M.N. and J.G. Armelagos (eds.). 1984. *Palaeoanthropology at the Origins of Agriculture*. Orlando, Florida: Academic Press.

Dahlberg, A.A. 1963. Analysis of the American Indian Dentition, in *Dental Anthropology* (D.R. Brothwell, ed.), pp. 149-177. New York: Pergaman Press.

Dahlberg, A.A. and K. Enoki. 1958. Rotated Maxillary Central Incisors, *Orthodontic Journal of Japan* 17: 157-169.

Furer-Haimendorf, C. von. 1945. The Problem of Megalithic Culture in Middle India, *Man in India* 25: 73-86.

Goodman, A.H., G.J. Armelagos and J.C. Rose 1980. Enamel Hypoplasias as Indicators of Stress in Three Prehistoric Populations from Illinois, *Human Biology* 52: 515-528.

Guha, B.S. and P.C. Basu. 1938. Report on the Human Remains Excavated at Mohenjodaro in 1928-29, in *Further Excavations at Mohenjodaro* (J.H. Mackay, ed.), pp. 613-638. New Delhi: Government of India.

Gupta, P. and P.C. Dutta. 1962. Human Remains Excavated from Megaliths at Yelleswaram (Andhra Pradesh), *Man in India* 42: 19-34.

Gupta, P., P.C. Dutta and A. Basu. 1963. *Human Skeletal Remains from Harappa*. Calcutta: Anthropological Survey of India.

——. 1970. Ancient Human Remains: Part I: A Study of the Nagajunakonda Skeletons, *Memoirs of Anthropological Survey of India* 20: 1-33.

Hawkey, D.E. 2002. The Peopling of South Asia: Evidence for Affinities and Microevolution of Prehistoric Populations from India/Sri Lanka, *Spolia Zeylanica* 39, 1-300.

Hemphill, B.E., J.R. Lukacs and K.A.R. Kennedy. 1991. Biological Adaptations and Affinities of Bronze Age Harappans, in *Harappan excavation 1986-1990: A Multidisciplinary Approach to Third Millennium Urbanism* (R.H. Meadow ed.), pp. 137-182. Madison: Prehistory Press.

Huss-Ashmore, R., A.H. Goodman and G.J. Armelagos. 1982. Nutritional Inference from Paleopathology, in *Advances in Archaeological Method and Theory, Vol. V* (M. Schiffer, ed.), pp. 395-474. New York: Academic Press.

Kennedy, K.A.R. 1975. *The Physical Anthropology of the Megalithic Builders of South India and Sri Lanka*. Canberra: Australian National University.

——. 2000. *God-Apes and Fossil Men: Paleoanthropology of South Asia*. Ann Arbor: University of Michigan Press.

Kennedy, K.A.R. and P. Caldwell 1984. South Asian Prehistoric Human Skeletal Remains and Burial Practices, in *The People of South Asia: The Biological Anthropology of India, Pakistan and Nepal* (J.R. Lukacs ed.), pp. 159-197. New York: Plenum Press.

Kennedy, K.A.R. and J. Levisky. 1984. The Element of racial Biology in Indian Megalithism: A Multivariate Analysis Approach, *Homo* 35(3-4): 161-73.

Kennedy, K.A.R., N.C. Lovell and C.B. Burrow. 1986. Mesolithic Human Remains from the Gangetic Plain: Sarai Nahar Rai, *South Asia Programme*, pp. 89. Cornell: Cornell University.

King, D.L. 1983. Etiology of Malnutrition, in *Dentition: Genetic Effects* (R.J. Jorgenson, ed.), pp. 83-94. New York: Alan R. Liss.

Larsen, C.S. 1997. *Bioarchaeology: Interpreting Behaviour from Human Skeleton*. United Kingdom: Cambridge University press.

Livingstone, F.B. 1991. On the Origin of Syphilis: an Alternative Hypothesis, *Current Anthropology* 32: 587-590.

Lukacs, J.R. 1981. Dental Pathology and Nutritional Patterns of South Asian Megalithic Builders: The Evidence from Iron Age Mahurjhari, *Proceedings of American Philosophical Society* 125(3): 220-37.

——. 1985a. Tooth Size Variation in Prehistoric India, *American Anthropologist* 87(4): 811-825.

——. 1985b. Dental Pathology and Tooth Size at Early Neolithic Mehrgarh: An Anthropological Assessment, in *South Asian Archaeology 1983* (J. Schotsman and M. Taddei, eds.), pp., 121-150. Naples: Instituto Universitario Orientale XXIII.

——. 1989. Dental Paleopathology: Methods for Reconstructing Dietary Patterns, in *Reconstruction of Life from Skeleton* (M.Y. Iscan and K.A.R. Kennedy, eds.), pp. 261-286. New York: Alan R. Liss.

Lukacs, J.R., M. Schulz and B.E. Hemphill. 1989. Dental Pathology and Dietary Patterns in Iron Age Northern Pakistan, in *South Asian Archaeology 1985* (K. Frifelt and P. Sorenson, eds.), pp. 475-496. London: Curzon Press.

Malhora, K.C. 1965, Human Skeletal Remains from Neolithic Tekkalakota, in *The Stone Age Hill Dwellers of Tekkalakota: Preliminary Report of the Excavations at Tekkalakota* (M.S.N. Rao and K.C. Malhotra, eds.), pp. 109-162. Pune: Deccan College.

Marrett, D.C. and S. Pfeoffer. 2000. Maxillary Sinusitis as an Indicator of Respiratory Health in Past Populations, *American Journal of Physical Anthropology* 111: 301-308.

Martin, R. and K. Saller. 1957. *Lehrbuch Der Anthropologie*. Band 1. Stuttgart: Gustav Fsher Verlog.

Mohanty, R.K. 2005. Some Important Observations: Excavations at Mahurjhari (2001-2004), *Man and Environment* 30 (1): 106-107.

Moorrees, C.F.A. 1957. Mesiodistal Crown Diameters of the Deciduous and Permanent Teeth in Individuals, *Journal of Dental Research* 36: 39-47.

Mushrif, V. and S.R. Walimbe. 2006. *Human Skeletal Remains from Chalcolithic Nevasa: Osteobiographic Analysis.* London: BAR Publications.

Olivier, G. 1969. *Practical Anthropology.* Springfield, Illinois: Charles C. Thomas.

Ortner, D.J. 2003. *Identification of Pathological Condition in Human Skeletal Remains.* (2nd Ed.). Washington, D.C.: Smithsonian Institution.

Ortner, D.J. and W.G.J. Putschar. 1981. *Identification of Pathological Condition in Human Skeletal Remains.* Washington, D.C.: Smithsonian Institution.

Pindborg, J.J. 1970. *Pathology of the Dental Hard Tissues.* Philadelphia: W.B. Saunders Company.

Potter, R.H.Y., R.S. Corruccini and L.J. Greene. 1981. Variance of Occlusion Traits in Twins, *Journal of Craniofacial Developmental Biology* 1: 217-227.

Rajan, K., 1990. New Light on Graffiti Marks, *Journal of Marine Archaeology* 2: 47-54.

——. 1991. Iron and Gemstone Industries as Revealed from Kodumanal Excavations, *Puratattva* 20: 111-112.

——. 1994. *Archaeology of Tamil Nadu (Kongu Country)*. Delhi: Book India Publishing Company.

——. 1996. Kodumanal Excavations – A Report, *Gauravam B.K. Gururajarao Felicitation Volume* (K.V. Ramesh, ed.), pp. 72-86. New Delhi: Harman Publishing Company.

——. 1997. *Archaeological Gazetteer of Tamil Nadu*. Thanjavur: Manoo Pathippakam.

——. 1999. Further Excavations at Kodumanal. *Man and Environment* 23(2): 65-76.

——. 2007a. The Earliest Hero stones of India. *History Today* 7: 118-122.

——. 2007b. Thathappatti: Tamil-Brahmi Inscribed Hero Stone, *Man and Environment* XXXII(1): 39-45.

——. 2008. Situating the Beginning of Early Historic Times in Tamil Nadu: Some Issuers and Reflections. *Social Scientist* 36(1-2): 40-78.

——. 2009. *Archaeological Excavations at Porunthal 2009*. Brochure, Pondicherry: Pondicherry University.

Rao, V.V., T.S. Vasulu and A.D.W. Rector Babu. 1996. Possible Palaeopathological Evidence of Treponematosis from a Megalithic Site at Agripalle, India, *American Journal of Physical Anthropology* 100: 49-55.

Reddy, N. 2002. *An Ethnoarchaeological Investigation into the Maxillary Sinusitis Pathology of the Chalcolithic Record*. Unpublished M.A. Dissertation, Deccan College Pune.

Reddy, Rami V. and B.K. Chandrashekhar Reddy. 1987. Human Skeletal Remains from Kodumanal, Tamil Nadu: A Craniometric Study, *Tamil Civilization* 5(1-2): 100-116.

Roberts, C. and K. Manchester. 1995. *The Archaeology of Disease*. Ithaca, NY: Cornell University Press.

Sali, S.A. 1986. *Daimabad 1976-79*. New Delhi: Archaeological Survey of India.

Sarkar, S.S. 1960. Human Skeletal Remains from Brahmagiri, *Bulletin Department of Anthropology*, 9: 5-26

——. 1972. *Ancient Races of Deccan*. New Delhi: Munshiram Manoharlal.

Sewell, R.B.S. and B.S. Guha. 1931. Human Remains, in *Mohenjo-Daro and the Indus Civilization, Vol. 2* (J. Marshall, ed.), pp. 599-648. London: Arthur Probsthan.

Stewart, T.D. 1979. *Essentials of Forensic Anthropology*. Springfield, Illinois: C. Thomas.

Trotter, M. 1970. Estimation of Stature from Intact Long Limb Bones, in *Personal Identification in Mass Disasters* (T.D. Stewart ed.), pp. 71-83. Washington D.C.: National Museum of Natural History.

Turner, C.J. II, C.R. Nichol and C.R. Scott 1991. Scoring Procedure for Key Morphological Traits of the Permanent Dentition: The Arizona State University Dental Anthropology System, in *Advances in Dental Anthropology* (M.A. Kelley and C.S. Larsen, eds.), pp. 13-31, New York: Wiley Liss. Inc.

Walimbe, S.R. 1993. Human Skeletal Remains from Megalithic Raipur, *Bulletin Deccan College Research Institute* 50: 667-678.

——. 1998. Bio-cultural Adaptations in Cranial Morphology among the Early Farming Chalcolithic Populations of the Deccan Plateau, in *Contemporary Studies in Human Ecology: Human Factor, Resource Management and Development* (M.K. Bhasin and S.L. Malik, eds.), pp. 25-40. Delhi: Indian Society for Human Ecology.

——. 1999. Pencil-sharpened Bones from India, (Jointly with C. Roberts) *Paleopathology Newsletter* No. 105, pp. 11-12.

——. 2007. Population Movements in the Indian Subcontinent During the Protohistoric Period: Physical Anthropological Assessment, in *The Evolution and History of Human Populations in South Asia* (M.D. Petraglia and B. Allchin, eds.), pp. 297-319. Springer: Dordrecht, The Netherlands.

——. *in press*-a. *Human Skeletal Remains from Banahalli*. New Delhi: Archaeological Survey of India.

——. *in press*-b. Palaeodemography of the Megalith Builders of South India, *Proceedings of National Seminar on Megalithic Traditions in Ethnography and Archaeology in India*. Bhopal: Indira Gandhi Rashtriya Manav Sangrahalaya.

Walimbe, S.R and S.S. Kulkarni. 1993. *Biological Adaptations in Human Dentition: An Odontometric Study on Living and Archaeological Populations in India*. Pune: Deccan College Research Institute.

Walimbe, S.R. and V. Selvakumar. 1998. Anthropological Investigations on an Iron Age Adult Male Skeleton from S. Pappinayakkanpatti, Madurai district, Tamil Nadu, *Journal of Human Evolution* 9(1): 19-34.

Walimbe, S.R. and A. Tavares, A. 2002. Human Skeletal Biology: Scope, Development and Present Status of Research in India, in *Recent Studies in Indian Archaeology* (K. Paddayya, ed.), pp. 367-402. New Delhi: Munshiram Manoharlal.

Walimbe, S.R. and P.B. Gambhir. 1994. *Long Bone Growth in Infants and Children: Assessment of Nutritional Status*. Mangalore: Mujumdar Publications.

Widdowson, E.M. and R.A. McCance. 1964. Effects of Nutrition and Disease on Growth, *British Dental Journal* 117: 326-330.

Wolpoff, M.H. 1971. *Metric Trends in Hominid Dental Evolution*. Case Western Reserve University, Studies in Anthropology.

Zuckerman, S. 1930. The Adichanallur Skulls, *Bull. Madras Government Museum* 2: 1-24.

Index